AF085297

Sandstone

SYDNEY UNIVERSITY PRESS

The University of Sydney Master of Publishing Program, the
University of Sydney in association with the School of Letters, Art
and Media and Sydney University Press
sydney.edu.au/sup

Individual authors © 2010
Sydney University Press © 2010
Cover design by Christian Cuello © 2010
Illustrations by Skye Starkey © 2010
Excerpt from 'The Engine Driver', The Decemberists, lyrics by Colin
Meloy © 2005.

Reproduction and Communication for other purposes
Excerpt as permitted under the Act, no part of this edition may be
reproduced, stored in a retrieval system, or communicated in any
form or by any means without prior written permission. All requests
for reproduction or communication should be made to Sydney
University Press at the address below:

Sydney University Press
Fisher Library F03
University of Sydney NSW 2006 AUSTRALIA
Email: sup.info@sydney.edu.au

National Library of Australia Cataloguing-in-Publication entry

Title:	Sandstone : Sydney University student anthology 2010 / University of Sydney's students.
ISBN:	9781920899677 (pbk.)
Subjects:	College students' writings, English--New South Wales--Sydney.
	Australian literature--21st century--Collections.
Other Authors/Contributors:	University of Sydney.
Dewey Number:	A820.804

The University of Sydney acknowledges the traditional owners of Country upon whose land the various campuses of the University now sit: Cadigal peoples of the Eora Nation, Deerubbin peoples, Tharawal peoples, Ngunnawal peoples, Wiradjuri peoples, Gamilaroi peoples, Bundjulung peoples, Wiljali peoples and the Gureng Gureng peoples.

Contents

Foreword
Matthew Reilly..1

The Voice
Edita Pahor..5

Sharpening Sticks
Daniel Jenkins..6

Far From the Wolfpack
Jimmy Andrews..15

A Considerate Sort of Man
Lauren Cammack..16

III
Tammy Wong...22

A Tuesday Night in June
Alison Gibson..24

In Praise of Feet
Nadia Menon..33

'Til the Boys Come Home
Agnes Bairstow..35

This Harbour
Theodore Ell..54

Circular Motion
Melissa Lee..56

The Incoming Tide
Suzanne Brown..59

Poets Don't Do Gym
Isabel Robinson...71

The Shady Side: Her Life in Taipei
Nadeemy Chen..73

Sunshine
Victoria Brookman...83

New Bones
Amy Brown..92

Panda
Amy German..94

Seagull
Amy German..95

Fourteen
Katie Henderson–Brooks..96

The Start
Connie Theresa Ye...98

Countdown to an Emigration
James Nathaniel–Grant...102

The Professor and the Poet
Tina Tin Lap Leung..117

Out of Egypt
Cathleen Inkpin...119

I Am a Writer
Conor Bateman...131

AT
Edita Pahor..135

In Stormy Visions
Elisabeth Murray...136

A Lovely Riverside Place
Mick Beltran..154

Bella May
Harriet Westcott..156

Environmentalism
Jimmy Andrews..162

Liz Goes to Beauty School
Nadia Menon...163

The Boy King
Michelle Retford...172

Supersized Me
Rebecca F Thompson..174

Ode to CityRail Suburban Carriages (K Set), Emu Plains to Chatswood on the Western Link
Kat de Jong..180

The Future of Books: From Gutenberg to Gadgets
Michelle Willoughby..181

Acknowledgements...192

Foreword

Matthew Reilly

It's the old catch-22. How do you become a published author? Well, you do so by being published.

Huh?

Let me put it another way. *The authors of the future need outlets through which they can be discovered.* They need to be found and we need to create ways for this to happen and this marvellous anthology is one such way.

(Believe it or not, my first paid, published work was for *Cleo* magazine. I sent in a sample article under the pseudonym 'Melissa Reilly', thinking that a female writer stood a better chance of being accepted; the editor liked my piece and called me ... and when they found out I was a guy, they were thrilled.)

And that's why I was pleased when I was approached to write this foreword.

Because the annual Sydney University Student Anthology provides an excellent forum for new writers *to be found*. Book publishers read anthologies just like this one, searching for writers they think might have the goods to write a book. They also check out magazines and newspapers.

If you want to have a novel published one day, it certainly helps to have been published in shorter form beforehand, whether in *Cleo* magazine, a student newspaper or in an anthology like this.

So I hope the writers featured in this anthology take great pleasure in knowing that they have just embarked on the journey to becoming a published author.

For every writer there is also the simple thrill of seeing something you have written published. Whether it's your name in shiny silver letters on the cover of a hardback, or your name in bold text atop a short story, it's a buzz.

So if you, dear reader, know any of the writers featured in this book, give them a hug, or buy them a beer, or maybe even dinner and a beer. This is a big deal for them. I'm thrilled for the writers who will see their names in print in this anthology because I know how it feels.

As for the works themselves, I'm blown away by how good they are. The writing is skilled, assured and refreshingly original—whether the subject matter is suicide or the Dreamtime and the Sydney railway network or the fact that poets don't do gym (the first poem in history, I imagine, about fitness professionals handing out gym flyers on street corners!).

I hope you enjoy the remarkable freshness, insight and cleverness that went into the writing of this collection as much as I did.

In the end, writers need to be discovered and I am sure that this anthology will reveal to you a few writers you might want to look out for in the future.

Happy reading.

Matthew Reilly is the author of several bestsellers including *Contest, Ice Station, Temple, Area 7, Scarecrow, Hover Car Racer, Seven Ancient Wonders, The Six Sacred Stones* and *The Five Greatest Warriors*.

The Voice

Edita Pahor

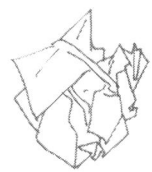

A torn piece of paper
Floats through the universe
'Don't worry', a voice says,
'I know it's yours—
I recognise your writing'.

Sharpening Sticks

Daniel Jenkins

As I stood in line, about twelve people in front of me, I decided I would buy a new pair of shoes. I noticed the kicks on the guy in front of me. He was wearing a brand new pair of Doc Martens, their shiny leather holding his feet like a glove. This was a serious pair of shoes. The wearer of the shoes didn't look much different from me: he was a young white male, maybe twenty-two or twenty-three, unshaven, and obviously unemployed. Yet, with those shoes on, I'm sure he could have conquered the world. Me, on the other hand: I was wearing an old pair of skate shoes that were only held together by a few rotting dabs of eight year old shoe goo, back from when I could be bothered to skate. Even the way he held his form—the only evidence of the jobs he definitely *didn't* apply for—showed a kind of confidence I was sure came from the shoes.

As the line shuffled forward again, I noticed the shoes on a girl towards the front. In fact, I noticed her first, then the shoes. She was causing a bit of a scene. She'd been lining up for over an hour, she yelled, her two year old was out in the car and she 'wasn't no mental case' like the rest of us. Everyone else in the line backed up, glancing awkwardly at each other. It was during this backward shuffle that I noticed the upset girl's shoes. They were white Dunlop Volleys, with a splash of dirty pink on the tongue. Looking at those shoes I became completely oblivious to the scene this girl was causing, and began thinking of my first pair of shoes, back when I was seven and about to embark on my first day of 'white man school'.

I wasn't a blackfella, still aren't, but I thought I was. That's not to say I was colourblind or anything, I could see my white sun-spotted skin like anyone else, it's just that I felt like I was black. Back on the island all the other kids had called me 'ghosty' or 'whitey' when we were playing, so there was no getting around the fact I was white, I just didn't think much of it at the time. To me, I was the same as they were, just maybe a bit clumsier in the water. It wasn't until I bought my first pair of shoes that I realised there was more to being 'whitey'.

On the island nobody wore shoes. Sure, we'd cut our feet on coral, pick up thousands of bindi-eyes, and get the odd shard of a broken beer bottle. But with the heat, the endless swims, and the huge amount of time spent either on grass or in sand, shoes just weren't really necessary. I remember when my sister was born my nanna sent over a little pair of baby shoes. Mum put them on Kate's tiny feet and we all watched as she ran up and down the verandah, not picking up a single splinter. I was four then and my feet were already tough as nails. I ran after her and showed her what a barefooted kid could do, by beating her to the far railing. She was only six months old but I think I proved my point. My parents, busy taking photos of my baby sister in her new shoes, didn't notice I'd won the race. So I sulked off to throw rocks at the green ants' nest with Tommy.

Tommy was my best friend and throwing rocks was our passion. We threw rocks at dogs, at teachers, at fish, possums and birds. We threw rocks at windows, tombstones and Coke machines. We threw rocks at the old ladies who sat drinking in the park, at the police as they rode through town and at the boats from Townsville which sometimes arrived at the jetty. We threw rocks at the people who got off the boats, who were always white and sometimes fat or blonde girls with video cameras or men in suits carrying clipboards. We even threw rocks at other rocks. And if we got bored with throwing rocks, we'd throw sticks, bottles, clumps of sand, shells, toys ... the list goes on. If there was one thing Palm Island—or my childhood for that matter—didn't lack, it was stuff to throw.

Tommy, like everyone else on the island—except the police, doctors and some teachers—was black. Unlike me, he actually was black, skin and all. He was about eight when it happened and I was six. I looked up to him like a god. He knew how to make spears out of Paddle Pop sticks. He could fillet a fish with nothing but a Coke can. We were at school one day, sharpening our spears on the cement in the quadrangle, when Tommy first mentioned the ghost dog.

'We'll get 'im tonight', Tommy said, looking up from the cement. 'We gotta kill this dog; he gone dare bin at me dad's chooks. Now me dad's away for a bit so we gotta get 'im.' Tommy ground his Paddle Pop stick harder and harder into the cement; it looked like it was about to snap.

'Easy dare, cuz', I said. I was always trying to be confident around Tommy. 'We set up some bait, fish or something, then we get up close 'n' spear it.'

'Won't work', Tommy said. 'Can't see it. It's a ghost.'

Since Tommy's mum died he didn't talk much, but whatever he said I treated as gospel. If he said there was a ghost dog eating his dad's chooks, he was right, and I was ready with sharpened sticks.

'A ghost, hey?' I said. 'We make a trap then.'

Tommy looked up again, a tiny glint of light in his normally vacant eyes. 'Reckon a trap would work?'

Of course I didn't know anything about trapping ghost dogs, but I could tell Tommy would be impressed if I did. 'Yep, we make a trap', I said, planning. 'We dig a hole, right? Then we put spears at the bottom of the hole like this, eh?' I showed Tommy how we could jam spears into the ground, pointy ends facing upwards. 'Then we cover the hole with grass or something. Then we make a line of meat or something leading up the hole.'

Suddenly Tommy's Paddle Pop stick snapped and he looked up at me seriously. 'Reckon that'll work?' he asked.

'I reckon', I said. 'Me dad shown me how.'

'Righto', Tommy said. 'Meet us at my place after school and we dig a hole.'

My dad had never really shown me how. Spelling and times tables, that's all I was taught. The reason I lied was that Tommy was always telling me about all the cool things his family had shown him. They used to go for trips to some of the islands where they'd hunt, fish, make fires. He'd even shot a gun. So I lied. Tommy knew words that I didn't, ways to describe stuff that I could never find the words for.

The hole was pretty deep by the time the sun fell into the ocean behind us. We filled the hole with our spears made from Paddle Pop sticks. It didn't look quite lethal enough so we got some XXXX longnecks from Tommy's rubbish bin, smashed the tops and threw the glass in. Now it looked like it could kill a dog, ghost or not. We threw in a few fish heads and placed some in a line leading up to the hole. Then we covered the hole with some spinifex and watched, waiting. Nothing happened. After about an hour we got bored. We decided to go down to the jetty and throw stuff into the water. There was so much stuff to throw at the jetty. I got hungry at about eight o'clock so I went home. Tommy stayed at the jetty, throwing old car tyres into the black ocean, and that was the last time I ever saw him.

I wasn't in trouble, Dad told me the next morning over breakfast, but we needed to have a talk. Tommy's father, Dad told me, had been seriously hurt overnight. I looked up from my bowl of Weet-Bix. Tommy's dad? This couldn't be good, I thought. But, as Dad told me what happened, I slowly realised that this wasn't just bad—it was the end of the world. Tommy's father, Dad said, had walked home from the canteen last night around midnight. He smelt something funny near the chook shed and went to investigate. On the way, stumbling blindly in the dark, he had fallen in a hole. The hole was full of sharpened sticks, broken beer bottles and fish heads. Tommy's dad wasn't wearing shoes. He survived, Dad told me, but he was pretty cut up. Not cut up enough, though, to not hobble inside and give Tommy a fairly serious beating. The neighbours heard the noise and the police were called. Tommy's dad was taken off to hospital and so was Tommy. Both were okay, Dad said, but we probably wouldn't be seeing them for a while.

I started crying. I said I felt sick and Dad said I didn't have to go to school that day. He took the day off, too. All day he did little nice things for me, and each thing made me feel worse. I couldn't tell him I'd helped dig that hole, that it was even my idea! No way. So, at the age of six and a half, I learned what guilt felt like. I didn't like it. But what could I do? Apologise? To who? Tommy's dad had gone back to prison; he'd been out on parole anyway and the prosecution said the 'mitigating circumstances' weren't quite mitigating enough. Having a foot full of Paddle Pop sticks and stinking of trout was no excuse to slap your son around. A few days later I walked over to Tommy's house and there was a man there in a suit, carrying a clipboard and touching things. I walked home. Later, Dad told me Tommy had moved to Townsville and was living with a foster family. Dad also told me that at the end of the school term we'd be moving, too.

By now the girl with the Dunlop Volleys had left. I was only about three people from the front. I couldn't stop thinking about her shoes; that splash of pink on the tongue. It was a similar splash of pink that made my first few months of my new primary school absolute hell. We moved from Palm Island about 1500 km south to a town called Armidale. My dad had a job as an Aboriginal liaison officer for all of the local public schools, and I had to go to one of them, so I needed a pair of shoes. Mum took me to a shopping centre. It was the first shopping centre I'd ever been to and my mind wasn't quite ready for it. What was I, a seven year old white blackfella, supposed to do in a place like this? Everything was either bolted down or encaged in glass, meaning nothing to throw. Lots of targets but no projectiles—even the rubbish was off limits, caged as it was in plastic bins. We went into

The Athlete's Foot and Mum told me to try on a pair of shoes. First she bought a pair of hard, leather school shoes for me to try on. No good. Then she had some black running shoes. I put them on and tried to run around. They hurt my toes. Just as Mum was starting to get angry I noticed a pair of black Hang Ten basketball shoes with velcro instead of laces. Having failed my lessons in rudimentary lace-tying, I decided I should give these a go. Mum agreed, probably just to get out of the store. When I put them on I noticed they had a shiny pink tongue. I loved that pink tongue, it reminded me of coral. I told Mum they were the shoes for me and we left, the secret of the pink tongue adding to my growing chest of secrets.

    I never told my parents of my involvement in the hole that sent Tommy's dad to prison and Tommy to Townsville. I still haven't. I tried my best to forget about it, but every now and again I was reminded of it, and my stomach would churn and my mouth would go dry and I wouldn't be able to talk. This happened on my first day of my new school, but it had nothing to do with Tommy or the hole; this time it was the fault of the shoes. I was going into Year Two halfway through the year, so all the other kids all knew each other and had formed groups, so it was up to me to make friends. At recess I saw a group of black kids playing handball on the cement. I walked up to them and showed them a sharpened Paddle Pop stick. One of them threw a tennis ball at me. At least they like throwing stuff, I thought, so I pulled out a bunch of Paddle Pop sticks I'd been keeping in my pocket and gave them each one.

    'Go on, la', I said. 'We'll make spears and throw 'em at those other kids.' One of the boys—the same who'd thrown the tennis ball at me—broke the stick in two and told me to piss off. All the others started laughing and saying 'Fuck off, whitey'.

On the island when people called me 'whitey' I didn't think anything of it, it was just a nickname, but here it was different. Here, for some reason, it hurt. Fuck them, I thought, holding back tears, and walked over to a bunch of white kids playing marbles.

'Can I play?' I asked. One kid, a bit older than the rest, grunted and chucked me a marble. It was a cat's eye; the worst kind. I knelt down in the dirt, feeling better, and sized up my path to the hole.

'Look at his shoes!' one of the kids yelled. 'They got pink on 'em.' The others looked down at my shoes. They all started laughing.

'Girl shoes, girl shoes!' they all chanted in chorus. Tempted to pull one of my spears out of my pocket and go to work, I decided it was best to just leave. I spent the rest of that recess behind the cricket nets, throwing spears into a rock. Lunchtime came and I went back to the cricket nets. I made spears from pine cones, sharpening them on the pitch. I spent the next four years of primary school like that—alone, making spears and regretting two things: the day I dug a hole and filled it with fish heads, and the day I bought girl shoes.

'Next', the Centrelink lady called and I felt that familiar churn in my stomach. I gave her my form and she looked it over. 'You actually applied for these jobs?' she asked.

'Yeah', I mumbled, my throat dry.

'Cleaner, dishwasher ...' she read over my form, looking up occasionally, 'bottle shop attendant, farmhand. You didn't hear back from anyone?'

'I dunno', I said.

She looked at me sadly, shaking her head. I handed her my medical certificate. She looked it over quickly then stamped my form. 'Your pay will be in tomorrow', she said. 'Next!'

    I walked out and got on a tram. Travelling slowly along Sydney Road towards the city, I realised I didn't really need new shoes. My old ones were fine. What I needed, I thought, was to throw something. I got off the tram and walked to the train tracks. There were rocks everywhere. I picked one up and threw it through the window of a forgotten warehouse. I didn't feel any better. I threw another.

Far From the Wolfpack

Jimmy Andrews

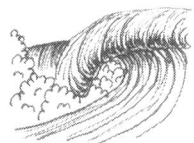

Awaking early and observing her
supple body stretch and turn and stir
from underneath a tossed, sweat-softened sheet
defies the *like* and *as* of cute conceit
and leaves me poised
                             the way a surfer stands
erect upon a shore of shifting sands,
sensing the ocean, permanent and pure,
seduce him with a spiritual allure
until—his State-fuelled fear of stingrays gone—
he dives in deep without a wetsuit on
and knows by the ensuing spray of foam
it's only in the swell that he's at home
since dissolution in its warm, wet whole
solely imparts completion to his soul.

A Considerate Sort of Man

Lauren Cammack

He was middle-aged with just the beginnings of a bald patch, barely noticeable, and for his lack of exercise he was not too overweight. He had done well at his job and was now in his fifth year as an area and shipping coordinator for the second-biggest hardware store in the country. He and his wife lived comfortably in the suburbs, with neighbours who bothered themselves to inquire about his health and who would mow the lawn if he was out of town for a weekend here or there. He had provided everything for his wife financially, and that mattered to him.

He did not love her.

He wasn't too sure when it had happened. He couldn't remember whether it had been gradual over the twenty-two years they had been married, or if he had simply woken up one morning unable to feel that particular sensation. Gone.

Just like that. A scooped-out vessel with red interior walls that glistened and breathed but experienced nothing other than mild hunger from time to time.

She was pretty, also middle-aged and worked two days a week at the local primary school's canteen. When she had insisted on getting a job there it had perplexed him. They had no children of their own—or any pets to take their place—and she had never worked with children in the past. He had seen it as a passing whim and believed eventually she would be back at home on Thursdays and Fridays to have his dinner ready when he returned from the office. It was not a passing whim, and dinner was always late at the end of the week.

He was sitting on the couch one Thursday evening, the sounds of chopping and sizzling from the kitchen blending with the television. He turned the volume up and scratched the side of his neck. It was a reality television show: a team of good-looking and deceptively good-natured people were renovating a lounge room and garden. A burly man was laughing and joking as he hammered together the platform for a swimming pool area. A thought sprang up in the man's mind.

While the man lay in bed that night the thought twisted, turned a little, and settled itself inside his head. Plans began to etch themselves roughly in his mind. It tickled and he felt excited at the thought of it—too excited. He looked at his sleeping wife, curled on her side facing him but out of reach. He took care of himself in the bathroom.

On Friday morning his wife left for the school, but the man was so thrilled with his new idea that he decided not to go to work and called in sick for that day, and for the following week. He would begin his project.

The materials were cheap. He knew all the distributors personally so the wood was very simple to get, even for the amount he wanted. He chose pine because it was strong and not too expensive. It had not been treated but that was okay because he was going to set it up in the garage at the side of the house. It was a large garage and with only one car between the couple there was plenty of space.

He sketched out the plans that day, ruler in hand and pencil running sharp. When his wife returned that night, he had already prepared dinner. She was surprised.

On Saturday he began to measure the wood. He had bought in excess, having completed the blueprint after the fact. He sawed through the pieces, his arm heaving like an iron jack, sawdust spraying out of the wound in the wood. The garage began to smell of the sawdust and he liked it; it was soft yet manly. That night he took his wife to the movies and though they barely spoke to one another, he shared his popcorn with her.

On Sunday the man mowed the lawn in the morning while it was still cool. The grass clippings spat out from the sides of the machine and filled the air with their sweet aroma. He waved at his neighbour, Rob, who was trimming the hedges. The beginnings of the frame for his project went up that day. The base, the legs, a few small steps, and soon it began to resemble the carcass of a stage. Decay in reverse. His wife was curious about his project but he smiled with good humour and said she'd have to wait and see. It was a surprise.

On Monday he lay down the platform of the stage. His hand jerked with the shots from the nail gun bolting down the planks. There was a problem with the middle of the stage so he added a few supports around the centre, or thereabouts.

Halfway through the day he offered to take his wife to the grocer and together they picked out what to have for dinner. They had grilled salmon, baked potatoes and a green salad. They hadn't eaten fish in years and he enjoyed it.

On Tuesday the man began the upper structures, but only managed to get two of the three vertical beams in place. It had been harder than he'd thought, having to do it by himself. Rob popped around briefly and they joked together. When he offered to help the man shook his head kindly and replied that it wouldn't be the same if he didn't complete it on his own. Rob shrugged and waved as he left. The man's wife was out that night and he found the house a little too quiet.

Wednesday came around and the man felt the excitement build. Only two more days and he should be finished. He lifted the third beam that day and bolted in the first of two crossbeams. He had never sweated so much. He managed in the second crossbeam and when he stood back, hands on his hips to survey his progress, he was pleased. That evening he layered on the first coat of eggshell paint, chosen because his wife liked that particular shade. He did it roughly, having a specific style in mind. The smell of paint drifted throughout the house and his wife inquired, but still he would not let her see. He chased her out through the hallway, laughing and tickling her, and she ran from him playfully.

On Thursday his wife returned to the school. He thought of the children she would serve that day, their tiny hands and faces eager for the food she would give. He felt a moment's disappointment that he had not given her children, but it was most likely too late now. Defects were too common in children conceived late in life. Adoption drifted across his mind but was gone before it seeded. The second coat of paint went on that morning and by late afternoon it had dried. He then sanded back the stage in spots, giving the whole thing a second-hand feel, like it was a beautiful antique piece he had found and restored himself.

He finished sanding after dinner and became covered in white flecks; snow in the garage, just for him. It speckled his hair greyish and made him look a little bit older than he really was. He joined his wife in the shower that night, to her surprise and delight.

Friday morning his wife woke late—exhausted from the unexpected night before—and rushed off to work still smiling. The man, leaning against the headboard with his hands cupping the back of his head, grinned at her as she left. He then rose and took a shower so long and hot his flesh pruned, and he could barely make out the skin-coloured blur in the mirror through the steam.

When he went into the garage he rubbed at his chin, examining his masterpiece. He kicked the side a few times but it was sound and did not jolt even a little. He skipped lunch, preferring a long and silent walk through the streets of his suburb. He waved at his neighbours and asked after their health. He invited Rob and his wife Erica over for dinner that night. They should arrive around six, when his wife was getting home from work. He told them he was surprising her and they smiled at his thoughtfulness. They hadn't surprised each other in a long time and resolved to do it more often.

At five o'clock the man went into the garage. The orange evening sun leaned in through the window but didn't offer much daylight. He flicked the light switch and the whitish stage glowed beneath the halogens. He took the four steps carefully, testing the tread of each as he went; everything had to be right. Nothing creaked.

When he was almost at the centre of the stage he took hold of the noose and slipped his head through. The rope was of fine quality and did not scratch his skin at all as he tightened it. He exhaled; proud he had finished and finished well.

His wife would be home soon. Rob and Erica would be here for her, as he had planned. Despite everything, he was a considerate sort of man.

JJJ

Tammy Wong

My dear, come be with me
We'll sit in secret silence
And muse on eternal tomorrows

Let the late afternoon be
       one long continuous handkerchief
       of loosely knotted squares
       of unconnected thinking what a surprise
That one births the other
from the deep pocket of my mind

Come think in thought-circles with me
Come find yourself in an intellectual cul-de-sac with me
Let's take the long way around the mountains
And have a picnic with complications

I rest in the hollow of your neck
And as the blow of infinity
Rushes by my ears
We sit in quiet solitary unity

A Tuesday Night in June

Alison Gibson

The days end quickly in June. Five o'clock hits and with the parade of workers making their way along the street comes the darkness. Variously coloured faces peer nonchalantly from train windows; the fluorescence inside the carriages is much more pronounced when the outside world is dark. An old man sits on a platform bench watching the peak-hour pedestrians. With hair that white and a scowl that severe, no one would dare deny him a seat. There's a girl in a work suit sitting next to him: dark skirt, bright green shirt visible under a tailored black coat, manicured nails texting without apparent thought on a slick mobile phone. She had paused briefly but noticeably before taking the seat, wondering if she would prefer to stand than sit next to such an old man. But she'd sat, leaving a carefully considered space between them so no unnecessary touching occurred. You could fit half a person in that space.

Winter nights are mild here; no frost-bringing chill in the air, despite the approaching rain. But at the moment when the sun disappears there is always an extra lifting of the wind. Reminding them all, perhaps, how lucky they are to be returning to the warmth of a house.

Not that the old man is going home. It's a Tuesday night: concert night. The lady at the ticket office last week told him, with far too much kindness for his liking, that if he were to go to the Saturday matinee sessions it would only cost fifty dollars—special pensioner price. He smiled his toothiest smile back and told her that his Saturdays were pretty busy and he'd stick to Tuesday nights. Perhaps she realised she'd offended him. Perhaps it was that his toothiest smile bore resemblance to a man twice his age, thanks to a childhood spent in Samoa and a lifetime of disregard of dental maintenance. Whichever it was, she flinched away and typed his reservation into her computer.

He checked his pocket now and felt the long, square column of cardboard that was the tickets. This was a nice ritual. Not every Tuesday, but once or twice a month, he'd buy two tickets to a concert; classical or old rock favourites, generally. Tonight was especially exciting: Simon & Garfunkel. The reunion tour when they had been reunited for years. But still, it felt new. He had been listening to their music when his peers were having children and struggling to keep up with who was the latest prime minister. 'April Come She Will' was played in the restaurant on his first date with Anna. 'American Tune' was played in the pub where she broke up with him three years later, sobbing her way through her desire for a family and his complete refusal to consider it. His last relationship. He smiled at the memory. Her Christmas cards still came, complete with updated photos of her and her husband, their now-grown children and the slowly expanding group of grandchildren. She looked happy. He'd never started the Christmas card tradition. He used to think he was missing out on all that space to brag, but now he is glad. They'd be getting emptier and emptier of news.

The train hisses onto the tracks in front of them. The girl beside him stands in a millisecond, priming herself for the peak-hour push into the carriage. He heaves himself to his feet, leaning heavily on his walking stick and waiting for people to make room. They do it dutifully, a girl roughly pulling her boyfriend out of the way and hissing, 'You're in the way, again'. The boyfriend looks embarrassed and gives the old man an apologetic smile. His expression remains still—that idiot of a boy doesn't need sympathy for sticking with a girl like that.

He sits at the back of the carriage, facing the other travellers. The couple who moved out of the way are getting cosy on a two-person seat, the girl nestled in nicely against the boy's shoulder. Maybe she's not so bad after all. There's a middle-aged man in a suit; on his way home from work, probably. His head is bowed and he looks tired. Because of his day at work or because of what he's returning home to, it's hard to know.

The train plunges through the night, rattling along straight then wobbling round a couple of corners. It stops, people leave. It stops again, even more get off. By the time it's nearing the old man's stop there is only the young couple, himself and a middle-aged woman left. The woman hasn't let her gaze venture into the carriage yet. Not wanting to make eye contact, perhaps, or just distracted by the flashes of scenery coming through the window. Either way, it lets him study her undisturbed. He didn't notice her in the throng of other passengers. Her hair is dark, but dark grey, he realises now. Her overcoat is black and looks heavy. It doesn't quite fit her, sagging into drapes down her front. Her face is calm but from where he sits she seems faintly embarrassed, her mouth set in a determined line. The avoidance of eye contact is definitely due to some hesitation, he decides. She doesn't want to know who is seeing her sitting there by herself.

The last stop before the stadium and a flood of people rush on, blocking his view of the woman. He starts watching his fellow concertgoers. A few young ones have come along, a couple of families. The majority are couples in their fifties or sixties, dressed smartly and holding hands. A few bars of 'At the Zoo' is whistled somewhere up the back and a few people laugh.

The train glides surprisingly smoothly into the station. The doors open and cold air bursts into the carriage—he'd forgotten how much colder it gets in the south of the city. Breaths are drawn in quickly and coats pulled tighter, bodies huddled in their hurry to keep moving. He stands slowly; no use fighting this lot to be first into the rain. The people move in a flurry of coats, excited voices and the occasional screech about the rain. The couple from earlier smile at him as they leave, their eyes brightly excited. He begins his move down the carriage and notices the embarrassed woman is still seated, although she's turned around and is watching the mass exodus. She catches his eye but her face remains passively curious. Her eyes are a deep grey, like her hair, and he notices a red blouse peeking out under her coat. He offers her an arm, old-gentlemanly style, and expects at least a smile in return. But she stands and accepts his gesture calmly, looking ahead out the doors and holding on to his elbow firmly. With a shock he realises that she thinks he needs help getting off the train.

They shuffle up the stairs and her grip tightens slightly as they step over the gap between the train and the platform. He grits his teeth. She must be barely fifteen years younger than him, older than his original estimate. In his head he tells himself to stop being stubborn, to let her think she's helping if she wants. He expects her to make some remark about it being an easy walk from here and to leave his arm and his side to go off on her own. But she matches his shuffling steps without restraint and he realises that she limps slightly, too. He's forgotten his umbrella. Well, really, he's forgotten to buy one for the last few years. Such a waste of space. His companion pulls one from her oversized brown bag, though, and holds it over them. They've yet to exchange a word, but somehow the silence has gone on too long now to need a conversation. They make their way towards the stadium.

As they approach the entrance he pulls out his extra ticket and offers it to her, his umbrella-lady. It's always handy having a spare. She pauses. Obviously she has her own ticket or she wouldn't be here, but he's hoping that the idea of walking in with someone instead of by herself is enough to convince her to come and sit with him. Plus, they're premium seats. She smiles her thanks and takes the ticket.

They enter the stadium and have their tickets scanned by a bright, young woman in a hideously patterned shirt; all browns and yellows and very unflattering. Good on her for still smiling, he thinks. They both head automatically for the lift and stand beside each other, waiting silently. Behind them a long-married couple is having a minor dispute over whether pre-show drinks are a good idea.

'But George, you know you'll just fall asleep. We spent a fortune on these tickets, can't we just enjoy it?'

'I won't fall asleep, Valerie, and it creates a nice atmosphere. A nice ... *ambiance.*' George says the last word with an overtly French accent. Valerie chuckles at the performance and gives in and they move away, towards the bar. The old man wouldn't mind a little tipple himself, but his date is already moving them into the now-open lift.

They find themselves seated four rows from the stage, which looms up larger-than-life in front of them despite being in darkness. He sneaks a look to the side and sees the reaction of his date is just as he'd hoped: wide-eyed and grinning at the improvement to her original seat. Her gaze moves over the stage in expectation. For anyone who has never been that close to a stage in a large auditorium before, it really is an overwhelming experience at first. Energy vibrates from the silent musical instruments, the guitars on their stands. The two drum sets up the back glisten in the half-light.

They've arrived just on time. Within minutes the house lights dim, the background music is silenced and a chirpy male voice informs the audience that the show is imminent and asks if they would be so kind as to switch off any mobile phones. His date dives into her bag in a flurry of nervous excitement and retrieves a heavy-set mobile; one of the first models, by the look of it. She fiddles with it for a few seconds before managing to turn it off. She is almost bouncing in her seat with the excitement.

The auditorium is large and dark and silent in expectation and the audience is not kept waiting long. Two unimposing figures walk out: one short, one taller with a distinctive silhouette of fuzzy hair. The crowd erupts as the stage explodes with light, illuminating the two figures so familiar and so nondescript. They stand together at a single microphone in the centre of the stage and the lights dim around them until there is merely a pool of light. The short one is carrying a guitar, which he now swings in front of him and begins plucking the strings in an ever-familiar tune. Their voices join in unison and carry up and over the cheers of the crowd. The old man forgets his date and settles back in his seat, letting the music pull him back to a different time of life.

*

There's no intermission. Two hours in and the old man's preparing to make a hobble for the toilet. They finish playing 'Cecilia' and he goes to stand up in the momentary silence but the lights—which had earlier exploded into full-on rock concert lighting—dim suddenly and he sits back down, worried about getting lost in the darkness. A spotlight picks out Garfunkel as he makes his way over to a piano complete with grey-haired pianist. The audience all know what must be coming. As the first few notes of 'Bridge Over Troubled Water' reach them, the old man senses a change in his date. He glances over and sees with surprise that her head is bowed and tears are cascading down her cheeks and into her lap. The crowd is silent, the atmosphere one of utmost attention. He doesn't want to speak; doesn't want to spoil the perfect symmetry between the music and the audience. So he places his hand on top of hers in her lap. She grips his hand tightly with both of hers, but doesn't turn to look at him.

He holds her hand and watches as Garfunkel strains to hit the high notes, sees in his face that Garfunkel knows this is the important one; the one everyone will remember and talk about later.

The song finishes and the crowd is on its feet. The old man and his date remain seated but are surrounded by able-bodied, standing fans and suddenly he can't see the stage. She turns to look at him, shaking her head and wiping away the tears. She stands and gestures at her tears in explanation of why she can't take anymore. He nods and takes her hand again, excusing them both as they shuffle past the still-standing fans. An usher spies them through the crowd and hurries down, making room and shining a torch at the ground so they can see. They get out of the auditorium and breathe in the cold air. He hadn't realised it was so stuffy near the stage. They walk slowly the way they entered, back down the elevator and out through the tall glass doors. The rain has eased and the tarmac of the road shines up at them as a black light. The sky has cleared and the air is clean, the refreshing taste of rain hitting their faces as they walk.

The train platform is empty when they arrive but the fluorescent screen tells them that a train will be departing in seven minutes, thirty-four seconds. He shuffles over to a seat. The cold has entered his knees and his painkillers are at home. The woman doesn't follow. She stands where he left her, staring out the train entrance at the clear black sky and the shining buildings. He leaves her be; he can almost hear the song being played again in her head. When the train arrives it screeches, but his ears are still slightly deadened from the concert. A conductor with a small purple turban and a heavy beard steps over to help him onto the train. The old man turns and sees the woman still standing, staring at the rain-soaked city. He wants to call out but he doesn't know her name. He waits, watching her. But he has the feeling she knows the train is there; knows that he is leaving. He moves into the carriage and sits down heavily. The conductor calls out to her, but there is no response. The doors sigh shut and the train jolts along the tracks. As the carriage pulls past, the woman raises a hand in a wave and blows a kiss before turning and walking out of the train station, her shuffle gone and her head high. He sighs heavily and leans back against the seat, wondering what concert he'll go to see next Tuesday.

In Praise of Feet

Nadia Menon

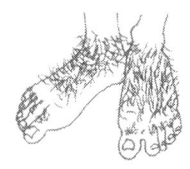

I like my feet.
So solidly dependable
Broad as—I don't know—
Bricks, a cricket bat, boats.
Unlike the rest of me
They can, if need be,
Be unmovable.
There's no hair on me toes
But, indeed, these are hobbit feet.
With cracked yellow soles they're
Tough as—what else?—
Boot leather.
Whenever the weather
Gets hot enough
I kick off whatever

I'm wearing,
The delicately sequinned,
Ridiculously strappy, flimsy constructions
That hurt.
Barefooted, my mind
Sits flush with the earth.
I spread my toes
In the dirt.

'Til the Boys Come Home

Agnes Bairstow

I meet Max the year I turn nineteen. At my full adult height I still have the narrow shoulders of a boy. I shave twice a week. I have two pairs of shoes and four shirts, but because I see hollow-cheeked men walking barefoot and on the susso, their boots slung around their necks, I do not think myself poor.

    I still live at home, travelling into town everyday on a train that belches smoke and stops with a steamy, juddering sigh that seems to mirror the discreet morning yawns of the passengers who quarter-fold their papers and hang their blazers from hooks on the wall. When the doors open, frosty air streams in. When the last people have boarded and the train speeds across the flat towards the city, the passengers light cigarettes and chat. The service carries booked seats and most people sit in the same carriage every day, as if this form of transport is less a necessity than a sort of moving club.

I listen to a group of men as they play cards, gradually fitting together a pointillist sketch of their lives from bits and pieces I hear over bets and scores.

—Mary's sister's pregnant again ... she wants to send the second eldest to live with us, bloody hell already got four ... my eldest wants to leave and start his apprenticeship ... Harry's teaching in Orange so he'll be all right for money.

These men speak with the ease of good friends, but when the engine draws hissing into the city platform they give quick goodbyes muted by a flurry of hats and coats, heading with half-grim faces towards jobs in buildings and warehouses.

I nod at these and other men and women, but I keep to myself and read. This form of friendship reminds me of my parents and their friends, less direct than people closer to my own age.

When I meet Max it is a bitterly cold July day, the wind so strong it hurts my teeth, my fingers cramping around the handle of my briefcase.

The lecturer's voice floats above the smell of wet wool and smoke. The usual first-day-of-semester rigmarole: we are asked to introduce ourselves to the people on either side of us. I shake the hand of a dark-haired woman to my left. Her hand is cool and her eyes smile briefly before she turns to the rugger-bugger who stolidly flanks her on the other side.

The young man to my right sits with the right shoulder of his blazer touching dark red brick. His handshake is firm, but the hand is very cold and I can feel gracile bones under the skin and muscle. I think of holding a bird in my hands as a child, not because I feel as if I am holding something delicate, but because the bones are right there beneath the surface, right beneath the warm skin and blood. It's strange. He stares at my chin, then his eyes meet mine and skate away across the room.

—Maximilian. Like the emperor.

I tell him my name and then, because he says nothing more and because I'm not sure what to say, the other conversations going on around us ebb forward. A young man sitting somewhere behind me chatters about jazz with the unwavering intensity of a fanatic.

I smile and Maximilian smiles as well. He has fair skin and light eyes. They flicker away again. It is a nervous movement, but he doesn't look nervous. Maybe he just wants to look at everything. Maybe he has never been in this room before and he is intensely interested by the windows, the old-fashioned tiles in the entryway, the smooth, bowed centre to each stair. I'm intrigued by his oddness.

The lecturer concludes his peroration and there is a great rustling of paper and shuffling of feet. As the conversation rises and I stand, I feel a hand on my arm.

—A beer? Some lunch?

I hesitate, surprised, and apprehension flashes momentarily on his face, quickly folded away and replaced with indifference.

—Yeah, okay.

We file through the door, down a corridor, outside. As my eyes adjust, the details of the life bustling about on the road seem very sharp and a little bit unreal, like the tiny scene you see when you look through the wrong end of a pair of binoculars.

There is a threadbare patch at the young man's elbow. A woman weaves through the crowd on a bicycle, a satchel slung over her shoulder. Near my feet someone stuffs library books into their bag. Maximilian squints, the winter air clear and clean now that the fog has burnt off.

—Now that we're more than acquaintances, you can call me 'Max'.

He concludes this announcement with another quick, flashing smile and gestures with his head as if to say, *come on*. I follow because I have nothing better to do and because I like this strange boy, who is my age but talks in a polite, slightly ceremonious manner that reminds me of my grandfather. There is a certain gentleness in it, deliberation, as if the way he speaks is a careful defence.

Max finishes his first schooner in four huge gulps, his face grim. I stare at the head on my own barely touched beer and wonder if this is a mistake. Max takes out a fag and leaves the packet on the table. I take one. The smoke rises above our heads and a group of men at the bar laugh raucously. I take another gulp of my beer and Max suddenly smiles, his eyes crinkling at the corners under sparse, sandy brows.

—That's gone straight to my head. Must be hungry.

Maybe that was what he was waiting for. He buys another beer and a plate of sandwiches and chats freely. He has a quick, dark sense of humour. He is more entertaining than I expected him to be, having readied myself for the chance that there would be a dry, donnish lecture where other people might expect a conversation.

Max is unlike my other friends. He doesn't have any of the raa-raa boisterousness of my schoolmates, the narrow enthusiasms of my university friends. He is physically remote. When he wants to emphasise a point he waves his finger in front of his face as if to say, *here, this is what I'm talking about*. When I draw attention to this mannerism he lets out a braying laugh.

The sense of his strangeness doesn't go away as I know him better and he seems to be aware of this. He has few other friends. When we talk about our families, childhood, things like that, Max speaks in a curiously indirect fashion. He'll say things like, *the house was at the end of the street, there was a park across the street* or *the poor bastard was shell-shocked at Ardennes I reckon, but God he could swing a cane.* To me these details come through as highly specific memories set adrift in a whole sea of things that Max will not share. It is as if he edits himself carefully for public consumption and I wonder how much care he takes to fashion this carefully expurgated version of his own life. There is art in it.

Occasionally, during a meandering conversation, I'll mention something that arouses a great cold anger, an impassioned rant. I never know whether or not I will spur on a heated debate.

I take Max home one night, for dinner. He engages my father in a long conversation.

—Corporations are too immoral, Max says. —We alienate business, looking upon it as something vulgar, something below analysis or science. Where is the morality in recession? Where is the science in depression?

We sit there, slightly stunned, over the mashed potatoes and the sausage. Where to begin? He leaves by the last train, a book borrowed from my parents' shelves in his hand. He seems happy enough, as if it's not the merit of the argument that matters but rather the chance to hone it on someone, see what they say about it.

—Quite an undergraduate argument, my father says. —Though he defended it well.

—Never mind what your father says, Mum says as she clears away the dishes. —I liked him. He seems sad, though.

I've never thought of Max as sad and I wonder about this. When I see Max next, I tell him about what my mother said.

—My mum reckons you seem sad.

—Really?

He shrugs, as if to say, *oh, I've never thought of that before.*

—Maybe you should use that to draw women in. Puppy dog eyes. They love it.

Max laughs softly and changes the subject.

A few days later, walking home alone from the train station in the dark, I think of another thing my father said. After he closed the door behind Max, he straightened up his bookshelves. He loves books, loves his library.

—Queer little fellow.

—Yeah, he is.

Now, walking home in the smell of wood smoke and cold, I think of what else my father could have meant.

I don't really know what Max is, although he is certainly sexually inexperienced. When I told him I had a new girlfriend he engaged me in a questioning session that reminded me of the whispered, snickering conversations that went on in the changing room at my school. It was the most normal conversation we'd had.

*

Max has a room in the city. One evening we get very drunk and instead of struggling home I fall asleep fully clothed on a narrow couch with the stuffing poking out of it. Apart from a bed and a bookshelf, this is the only furniture in Max's room.

In the morning we rise and stagger around in shared misery. The landlady has a wireless downstairs and I can hear it crackling.

—Oh, God. I need greasy food.

—I need a bath.

Max takes a towel and a shaving kit and goes down the hall. I hear him calling to the landlady in his clipped, polite way. Water sloshes and I hear the bathroom door open. He sings out.

—You can look at my books if you're in need of entertainment.

He speaks as if he's offering a library with leather spines and soft, dimpled chairs, instead of a lumpy couch and disordered piles. I light a cigarette and feel awful. To take my mind off the regretful, bilious feeling in my guts, I have a look at Max's books. A few have his initials on the flyleaf, but not all. I put down a copy of a book about the HMS *Bounty* because the small type makes me feel sick and I pick up the next book on the pile, *A Handful of Dust*.

There's an inscription on the first page below the title, what my father calls the frontispiece-facing endpaper. *To My Dear Son Max, on the Occasion of His Fifteenth Birthday.* I have read the book and to me it seems a singularly strange gift for a boy. Why not *The Boy's Own Book of Woodworking* or a stamp album? The handwriting is clean and neat and regular and it seems more sterile than the print itself, the words cold.

I riffle through the pages, still thinking of this, smelling clean paper. A photo tumbles out. A tall, thin man with a narrow smile, holding a towheaded child wearing shorts and a woollen vest, his arms linked together around the child's midsection. The child is Max.

I realise what the room is missing: photographs. Max has just this photo, closed into a book and soft at the corners as if it has been kicked around.

I close the book and put it back, feeling as if I've violated something through revealing that Max's careful reticence about his family conceals the fact that he has no photographs proudly framed, no care packages from home. No love.

Later on I say, —You never told me where you grew up, you crafty bugger.

Trying to sound jocular.

—Boring suburban upbringing, mate.

He elaborates, talking about primary schools and a backyard, a dog. I sense concealment and change the subject. If Max wants to lie about his family, that's his business.

*

I have a long break between lectures on Tuesdays. I spend it reading in a quiet corner of the library. I'm making careful notes on a textbook chapter one day when Max slams a small pile of books down on the desk.

—What do you want?

I put down my pen, a little bit annoyed. Max plucks at the page.

—What's that you're reading? Economics, God. False science. It's all guesswork. They throw up their hands and write a textbook about it.

I cross my arms and lean back. The chair creaks.

—Shhh. There are people studying here.

A woman at a nearby table looks up disapprovingly.

—If you want to rant about it let's go outside.

I incline my head in the direction of the woman, who spends a heartbeat dripping scorn at Max then props her head on her hand and returns to her reading.

—I wasn't ranting.

—Yes you bloody were.

Max sits down on the floor, his back to a metal shelf. He closes his eyes. I notice that his hands are shaking, cradled in his lap.

—What's wrong? You sound funny.

I'm half-whispering. He doesn't say anything for a little while; taps his finger against the sole of his shoe.

—Can I have a smoke?

He lights his cigarette and shakes out the match, blowing out an angry stream of smoke. He puts the pile of books under his arm, since you're not supposed to smoke in the stacks. We go out into the corridor. Max goes to the window, turns around to look at me.

—Ever wonder what you're doing?

He turns his head to look down on the path below. I jingle the coins in my jacket pocket, the metal cold against my palm.

—Not really, no.

—What do you mean, 'not really'? Either you do or you don't.

A librarian pushes a squeaky trolley piled with books. Max turns around from the window, takes a last drag and drops his fag in the sand ashtray by the door.

—In the way you mean … no. Not in the way you mean.

I watch a little blue line of smoke rise from the ashtray.

—Yeah, well. You're a lucky bastard, then. I hate this place.

—That's a bit melodramatic.

—I want. I want to be happy like you are. You know, just doing one thing.

It's as if I stand with my feet firmly anchored to the ground and Max can't help but jump from place to place. A teaching job in my future, maybe a foray into academia. And Max uncertain, wavering from week to week. So many young men like him. What worry is there in my future? None of the chaos of Max's life. No petty human affairs, no messy affairs or divorces for him, but always uncertainty, an axis always threatening to wobble off course.

Max takes a deep breath and scuffs his shoes against the lino.

—Do you think there'll be a war?

—Dunno. My dad thinks so.

We speak in the conversational tone of boys who have no real memory of the war, its horrors.

But at the same time, because we are young men, we ache to prove something. If we are asked to go, too few of us will hesitate. Both of us plan to go for the Air Force.

*

Sometimes I can only afford one beer. Since Max has more money than me, and I don't want either of us to be embarrassed, I spin it out as long as I can. We're sitting in a beer garden one day, one of those long, beery conversations, and I bring up childish nightmares. My older brother told me, the baby of the family, about a local child who long ago caught tetanus by jumping on a rusty bed. He was as stiff as a board when they found him, my brother said, and I lay awake all night scared stiff myself. I imagined a bedspring unfurling creakily to scratch me and doom me to die, immobile, of tetanus. I confessed these fears to my father in a welter of tears probably caused by lack of sleep.

Max throws back his beer. His second, my first. I wonder if he realises I'm just as thirsty as he is.

—I had a dream about a man.

—Scary man?

—Yeah. And one night I had a bad dream, this man was chasing me. So I sung out and my dad came to the bed and he said, *Son, it's all in your head. Now I want you to close your eyes and imagine yourself holding a big, black, gleaming gun. And when that man comes for you, I want you to shoot him.*

—Jeez. That's ... did you?

—Yeah.

There's a pause. I finish my beer. My mouth is full of the bitter, malty taste of it. The beer garden smells of smoke and beer and wet soil. Max rattles the box of matches in his pocket, silent.

—We're so needlessly cruel to the things we create.

Weeks later, he mentions that he has had a letter from London. From his father.

—What's he doing in London?

—He lives there.

—Oh, I say. —What does he do?

—He fucks around with his bohemian friends, most of whom worship him as a literary prophet.

Max speaks in the same quiet, controlled tone he always uses. He puts his hands in his pockets. But he spits out the word 'bohemian' with a sneer in his voice, as if it leaves a bad taste.

—He's a professional shit. In his spare time he writes.

I say nothing. Max goes to his wardrobe and takes out a box, throwing aside a few old pairs of socks (nobody to mend them). He upturns the box. Pristine, first-edition hardcovers: an author who has been praised for his vision and the clarity of his prose, awarded prizes. Each is signed: *To Max, my son.*

I think of the biographers and the magazine feature writers who have written about this man. How do they smooth over this treachery, this angry, abandoned son, the absent wife? Maybe they quietly mention, as an aside, that the literary prophet is *flawed*. As if something so superficial, an imperfection in the grain of a life, could account for what I hear in Max's voice. I wonder how it feels to be an aside, a footnote.

*

We walk in the park one morning. It's spring now and the grass is so green it looks unreal, like a film. There is a grassy smell in the air, the good old English flowerbeds already wilting in the heat.

—God, Max says. —I feel restless.

—It's the spring, I say. —You need a root.

—Dirty bugger. I need to get away from this city.

—My aunt and uncle have a place on the coast. I could ask to borrow it. Drive down and go for a bushwalk, camp.

—I've never been camping before.

—Really? What did you do on holidays?

He puts his head back, trying to remember something. Not a cloud in the sky.

—I have a vague memory of a hotel room somewhere. We never really went anywhere on holidays. We went places so my father could *work*.

—Okay, that's it. We're going away.

I'm initially worried that Max will have a heretofore concealed prissy streak, no bush sense. But he goes through the packing and bushwalking experience with a sort of innocent wonder. He asks what things are used for, whether we'll see any wildlife, how far it will be. He remarks on the sharp hot smell of sun on eucalyptus leaves, a smell that makes me think of home. I show him a topographic map and as we walk in the national park I teach him the basics of navigation. We camp one night and then walk back out, sweaty and triumphant, to the small beachside house that belongs to my aunt and uncle. We change into swimmers and plunge whooping into the surf. It's still cold this time of year, so we don't stay in for long. The house is fibro and it smells of dust and hot bitumen. We pull on clothes that smell of wood smoke and sweat.

We eat canned food and then we go down to the beach and light a fire. Max squirts on more lighter fluid than is necessary. Then he goes up to the house and comes back with a bottle of whisky.

—You carried that the whole way?

—That's what you do on the beach, right? Sip whisky out of the bottle?

It tastes awful to me, but after awhile the taste ceases to matter. We lie back with the sky purple above us. There's a rushing in my ears and it seems that right after that we're lying in the dark.

—Whoa, I say. —I'm as pissed as a newt.

We talk shit for awhile and laugh. Max takes his shoes off, wiggling his white city-dweller toes in the sand. He pokes at the fire with a stick. He takes my pocketknife from where it sits with the lighter fluid and newspaper. He opens the largest blade, closes it again.

—Watch it, I say.

The firelight glints off the blade.

—That's sharp. You could cut yourself.

As I form the words my mouth feels strange, as if the mechanism connecting thought to action has become stretched, ineffective.

He opens the knife and keeps it open. I wish I weren't so drunk.

—Max?

—Yeah.

He turns the knife around in his right hand, so it points directly at his chest. Something cold drops to the bottom of my stomach. He takes the knife and puts it under his singlet and for a second I'm filled with an electric, all-encompassing dread. Then the point rips through the fabric and he pulls it downward. I watch. I can't speak.

—This is my skin, he says.

He carefully folds the knife and places it back on the sand. Widens the tear until a huge strip is created. He pulls with both hands until his singlet hangs off him as if through a new, rather large, neck hole. He stands and it drops at his feet, destroyed. He's quite thin; I can see a small point of darkness in the hollow above his collarbones.

Max walks slowly towards the surf and stands there knee-deep, his trousers wet. Then he cups water in his hands and sluices it over his head. He calls to me, quite jolly.

—This is fun. It's cold. You should try it.

I walk down to the surf.

—Max, please, come out.

The cold thing in my stomach hardens. I feel a bit sick.

Max comes out of the surf and I remember nothing else of that night except that at some point, unconnected to any other time, I vomit in the sand right next to the dying coals. There is a greasy smell of naphtha and seawater and smoke, and all of this—the rushing of the sea, the taste of the whisky, Max's discarded shirt crumpled in the dirty moonlight, his voice—seems to seethe up around me. I lie back with my head palpably spinning and the next morning we both wake up on the sand, our mouths dry, covered in stale sweat. We bathe in the sea again and drink draughts of cleansing tank water from my aunt's kitchen, and then we go home.

*

The end of the break is four weeks away when Max asks me if I would like to mind his room. It's a good room and the landlady doesn't mind as long as the rent gets paid. I've been working, roughening my hands earning a pittance, so I agree to look after the place until Max returns at the beginning of semester.

—Then I can start looking for a place of my own, I say to Max. He smiles briefly and goes on packing.

After a week I get a postcard from the country. The usual tourist chatter. *The country is beautiful. Might stay away a while longer.* Max has met a young man who goes to the University of Adelaide. The young man has a car and they go touring together, dropping in at wineries and snapping photos. It sounds idyllic. I write back, chattering about the mundane stuff of my life. I inspect another room. I go to work. I read. I go out with my friends. I see a woman I know from a tute. When I hear a joke that I know Max will love, I jot it down.

I find a stick book between the box spring and the mattress when I change the sheets. I try to replace it in the same spot.

Max sends another letter, supplying a boarding house in Adelaide as his address. More of the same. *Adelaide is hot.* He gives me the name of a woman in the outer suburbs. *If you have any problems with the room, write to her.* I can't imagine what the problem could be but I write anyway, telling the woman that I am a friend of Maximilian's, that he has gone away. In the second draft I replace 'wandering' with 'travelling'. Then, feeling servile, I ask if the woman has any instructions. I assume that the woman is his mother.

The reply comes a week later. *My sister's son is not my concern*, the letter reads. Not 'my nephew' but 'my sister's son', as if Max's aunt is trying to divest herself of any form of responsibility. *If you have trouble paying his rent, cash one of his father's cheques.* I draft an angry reply scolding this woman for thinking me a bludger. Then I realise that the most wounding thing in the letter is that the tiresome, nagging woman (there is a whinging tone even in her written communication) doesn't care. I crumple it up.

Letters for Max have arrived: a long cream one with a Royal Mail stamp on it, a couple from the university. I pile them neatly on the bookshelf. It's then that I notice that Max has taken a few books with him, including *A Handful of Dust*. But why should I suspect anything? I have a comfortable room in the city. My friend sends cheerful letters full of witty observations.

There is a feeling of floating about these weeks, as if I am suspended, waiting for something. There is a cosy sense of complacence.

Another letter from Max arrives, written on thin notepaper. The tone is strange. *Thank you for being such a true friend*, Max writes. *I have made friends out here. Some of them are not so kind.* I put the letter away in Max's desk drawer with the rest of our correspondence, but I can't stop thinking about it. As I lie back in his bed, staring at the ceiling, Max's spare phrases echo through my head. *You can open my mail, if you wish. I don't mind.*

I sort through his mail until I find the letters from the university. I open them both. One is a terse notice about overdue books. The second letter is a longer one, confirming Max's application for a leave of absence and wishing him luck in his endeavours.

I thought I trusted you, I think. But I have no right to feel cheated. Why should Max include me in his plans when I'd only try to make him stay?

Max, what are you doing? As I write, I get angrier. *If you want to fuck around on the other side of the country, that's fine. Take some of your father's money.* I send the Royal Mail letter to Max, unopened.

Every week I hear a little more about the war. Conscription and rationing and munitions. A cartoon above the letters page shows a dark presence unfolding itself across Europe and towards Australia. The discussion among my peers is always focused on the future: houses, children, jobs, or a uniform and a ship to somewhere. How dare they, some of my friends say. *We must ... you've got to ... I refuse to believe it ... there's another solution ... join up.* So much talk and we all see the future in two narrow horizons.

Max sends back a letter written in longhand on notepaper. He has sent a money order and I cash it without embarrassment. He starts out with more chatter. He tells me about the sun setting through the spires of the churches, dusk in another city. Then with a sort of resignation he says, *I'm sorry. You're not the type to run away, but I am.*

I am no longer frustrated with Max's evasive obfuscations. I am confused. Running away from what? I leave Max's room and walk around, the soles of my shoes thin, a sort of dull roar in my ears. Why run, Max? What are you running from? I begin to realise that Max sees everything differently. If I could tilt the world ninety degrees, change the way I perceive things, maybe I would begin to understand.

Weeks go by. I clip an article about war preparations out of the paper and send it. The war is no longer an abstract thing. It's coming, it's just over the horizon.

I wonder whether Max would feel suffocated, living as I do. I go to the art gallery one afternoon, on a whim. I walk down through the park and through the quiet galleries and I see things that make me think of Max. A group of young men and women talking. So much talk. Passionate, carelessly articulate. Something about the quiet genius of the galleries, the earnestness of the students who loiter on the steps, makes my chest ache. The work. The sense of urgency in their searching, grasping conversations. How many of these young men will destroy themselves?

I buy a postcard and send it to Max.

Shoot him, I write. *Shoot him, and then come home, and we'll talk about it. Your father, whatever makes you think you cannot face this awful future straight-on.*

I wait for a reply. The world shuffles on, to the war, and I wonder who among us will survive it.

This Harbour

Theodore Ell

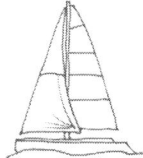

A sensing channel that inhabits itself,
an opening for lifetimes to leave tide-marks
on shores drawn tighter by riveted bridges
compressing millions to a fractal handprint,
the life-line rippled through bow-waves, keels and wakes.

A wild that charts itself by waterfront art,
the ocean kilometred, navigating
the settling way upriver to government
through the stations of pontoon and balcony
and scaled to the city with its benchtop cliffs.

Offices cube as myopic lighthouses,
homes crowd to greet the liners they bought views for
and cringe behind bush reaches for the tankers,

but the stately ones refrain from turning blind
and grow verandahs on their headland gardens:

remembered rigging and flag masts are enough
and Denison's daily cannon knock at one
hailing the other punctuation islands.
Serried ferry passengers watch picnickers
wondering if they share the commuters' ache:

new days clambering over South Head skylines
spill an ultimate sunrise, as when a love
in the dark is seen at last with the light on,
but stays only when business does not get round
to correcting the accident of beauty.

A yacht maturing turns anchored to daylight
awaiting a crew—so ready, so ready—
looks west, to the barrier, the sandstone gaps,
altitudes of heat and urban tectonics:
ridge, paddock and spread, houses between houses.

Circular Motion

Melissa Lee

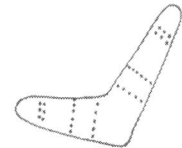

I live in Beecroft. A respectable thirteen stations from Redfern. *Don't be seen there.* I'm unsuitably dressed for the venue, they tell me. *Disgraceful.* The colours are all wrong.

My parents don't speak of the past. They're engineers, so they live in the future—blazing trails of maths and mechanics. Secure in the simple linearity of progress. They are speeding arrows, flying straight and true, without a backward glance. *There's nothing for us there.* I'm not an arrow, though.

Then ...?

An abstruse projectile ... with a flight fashioned always to return ... to seek the hand that set it free.

Now it's calling me back.

I see ghosts. Wisps of something unnamed, wavering vaguely in the dark so they blur at a touch. As spectres on a moonless night they tell of tales unspoken. Of a question. Or a desire?

I'll quench it.

Next stop, Redfern. Stand clear, doors closing.

*

There's something in the dotted whorls of red and white and yellow which swirl beyond the edges of mounted canvas on display. Mystery hides within these circles. Their painter is a huddled mass of grey hair and dark skin melded with the shadows of the modest art stall. Her peering eyes say nothing of the drug abuse or violence that claim this town's disrepute, but reflect the joy and sorrow of a time forgotten. They are the eyes of a people separate from the addicts and dole bludgers echoing from my parents' tongues.

I point to the painting: 'Is there a story?'

A sudden light is spreading across her face. *Our people are good storytellers.*

Now the ghosts take form. Breathing life from her words, they swell with colour and song. They dance as corroboree music drums the flight of an emu under chase, and they creep stealthily with the hunters downwind of a kangaroo; boomerangs and nulla-nulla poised. I laugh at the sight of swollen Tiddalik and marvel at the trail of the Rainbow Serpent. I tiptoe reverently past the rock dwellings of the tall Mimi spirits and am careful not to wake the bunyip dozing in his billabong. The old woman sings words I don't understand, but with meaning written in my being. Then we gasp as a tiny skink leaps from her cupped hands, and smirk, hoarding grubs and berries safely beyond reach of the women with their dillybags. Above us orange flame stains the milky azure and finally melts into smooth darkness. A whistle shrills from the station.

Stand clear, doors closing.

*

The train runs fast tonight, speeding me home, thirteen stations away—back to where I started. But I've returned from somewhere much further. I've come home to two beginnings.

I step through the door, embracing the parents I've not seen for a day. Later I will hang the painting on my wall, embracing the elders I've not known for a lifetime. I'll take my place in the smoky circle of the old bora ring beside my ancestors from the Dreamtime.

Where it all began.

The Incoming Tide

Suzanne Brown

It all began on a blistering, bright day when we went to the beach as one family and returned as another.

We'd come to our favourite bay for snorkelling. Mum, Dad, my sister Penny and I were to meet with my Year Eight classmate, Angus, and his dad, Jeremy. On clear days muscular silver snapper and googly-eyed squid swam among the swaying seaweed. On this day the ocean was soapy bathwater and we couldn't see more than half a metre in front of us.

Penny drove us there in the family station wagon. She desperately wanted her P-plates so pressured Mum and Dad into letting her drive. Mum sat in the back with me. When the car crested the final hill we could see the turquoise sea. Today, though, Penny didn't just coast—she planted her foot so the car spurted forward.

'Slow down, you idiot!' shouted Dad, grabbing the dashboard.

'Don't call your daughter an idiot', Mum said.

'So this is how you taught her to drive; all calm and Zen-like while she ploughs into another car?'

Mum didn't respond. Dad looked straight ahead. I could see the small blueberry-like vein that bulges from his neck pulsing. It exasperated him that Mum refused to argue. I'd witnessed enough times when Dad had let forth a string of swearwords and Mum had ignored him, coolly adding an item to her shopping list.

Mum's silence got to me sometimes. I wanted to fight with her when I got home on school days when I felt stiff from sitting at a desk and teary because a friend had left me out. But Mum never got riled. It made me want to throw a plate against the wall, like we'd done in a Greek restaurant. Dad once threw a coffee mug. It dented the wall before landing on the carpet unbroken.

Dad's voice would go from talking to yelling in a sentence. He often swore although he apologised later. Mum didn't have to apologise for saying nothing. But somehow I felt they were both wrong. I wished they had less of themselves and more of each other.

The gentle swell of the sea mirrored Mum's exterior that day. Clouds thinly covered a scorching sun. Penny and I had been given new rash vests for Christmas so we lathered the backs of our legs with sunscreen.

It was rare to have both Penny and Dad in the water. Penny didn't like to be separated from her mobile phone and Dad liked his weekend papers.

We had been snorkelling close to the rocky shore in a large loop and had stopped not far from where we'd jumped in, which I suppose is why Dad was with us. Dad goes kilometres out to sea if he's on a fishing boat, but when he snorkels he doesn't venture far.

Dad was swimming near Angus, about ten good strokes away from the rest of us. I had stopped snorkelling to adjust my goggles. I saw it first. Jeremy jerked his head around to follow my gaze. There, maybe fifty metres away, was a fin. That's all you could see: a dark grey fin, gliding through the water with barely a ripple in its wake. It was coming towards us, moving in a lazy, swaying way. And then it went under the water.

I felt warm urine in my bathers. Mum sucked in a breath. 'Oh lord', Jeremy said. He raised an arm as though he was preparing to punch it. I couldn't move beyond simply staying afloat. There was the sense that my legs, cycling away in the water, were somehow drawing the predator towards me.

The fin reappeared a few metres away and did a little jump and dive and kept going out to sea. Only then did I register the silent crowd that had formed on the shore. Among them was Dad.

And so began our family jokes: that Dad swam off and Jeremy threw himself in front of us to save us from the shark-turned-dolphin. In reality, Jeremy probably froze just like we did, but it was more fun to portray him as the white knight of the sea.

On the beach afterwards we were all laughing, except for Dad, his head back in his papers. I hugged Jeremy, Angus, Mum and Penny. It felt as though someone had shaken me and all my particles had settled back in a different order. I felt stronger and my homework didn't seem that important. Penny flung her arms around Jeremy and gave him a kiss. Mum laughed a lot, too. We all sat in a row and then we laid back on the warm sand like toddlers. I closed my eyes and the world glowed orange.

Whenever I thought of that day I always thought of it as a shark. The whole time it was coming towards us and had gone underwater I had thought it was a shark. I can remember thinking that I had never kissed Angus and that my friend Tina owed me three dollars.

I thought a lot about Dad getting out of the water. He'd been such a tough father. Yelling at us if we irritated him; threatening to get out the strap. The flipside of this was his affection: sitting us on his lap long after we had grown out of it; covering our faces with kisses when he returned from a fishing trip. He'd been strangely tranquil since our close encounter with the dolphin. He'd been neither angry nor soppy. Perhaps he was thinking about what kind of man leaves his wife and children to face danger on their own. I don't think I was the only one who pondered this question. Dad and Jeremy had both been cast in a new light and they knew it.

Angus and Jeremy visited our house a lot after that, both together and separately. They didn't knock; they just wandered in through the coloured plastic fly-straps. Angus's mum, Kathleen, never came because she was sensitive to smell. All of their clothes had to be washed in a special fragrance-free powder. Once when I went to Angus's house after school Kathleen said my hairspray made her feel ill.

My friendship with Angus went back to an after-school detention. His detention was for yelling during a test and mine had been for having a mobile phone in class. It wasn't even my phone; I was passing it to Claire.

After detention, as we were unlocking our bikes, Angus said, 'Mr Shepard takes everything a little too seriously, don't you think?'

'Oh yeah, he's always talking about respect and obligation.'

'And doing a test every week; no other teacher does that.'

'He's the opposite of Mrs Pickles; she doesn't even do a roll call.'

I'd never felt as relaxed with a boy as I did with Angus. I had no brothers and no male cousins. Just Dad and his brother, Uncle George, and they were both solitary and serious.

Penny had no boyfriend, even though she was in Year Eleven. Mum and Dad were intent on her doing well in her final two years at school, so they limited her socialising. Now, though, things were different. Penny started to stay up late lots of nights, playing cards with Mum and Jeremy. I think Mum wanted Penny to go to bed, but Jeremy always said, 'No, she's okay, let her stay'. I wished that Angus came around as much as Jeremy.

Dad was home less and less. He said he had to help Uncle George at the fish markets. That the nursery where Dad propagated tree seedlings needed him to work extra hours delivering rosebushes.

Dad loved nature, so it had been hard for him to move from the country to the suburbs. When Mum and Dad had married they had bought an almost treeless block of land on the outskirts of Sydney. Dad had planted six gum trees, which threw shadows and bark over the house. The largest stood in the right-hand corner of our front yard. It had a girth of two metres. It looked as though the tree had pushed through the earth in its current size like a huge steel pylon. You had to look way, way up the trunk to see the branches and leaves. From the ground the branches looked like a road you could travel down: wrong turns which could've been the tree's mistakes, instead of going straight ahead on the one path. These wrong turns could drop when the wind came up and you'd hear a loud crack, followed by a thud. 'Widow makers', they called these huge gum trees.

Sometimes after school I would lie on my back under the tree with Angus, looking at the creaking canopy.

'The roots spread far wider than those branches', Angus said. 'They spread right under your driveway and into the next door neighbour's yard. The tree has tongues where its feet should be.'

'Are they soft like our tongue?'

'No, they're like bones.'

'But how do they move?'

'So slowly you would never see it even if you could peel back the grass.'

'Huge dish mop', I said, looking back at the tree's canopy. There were no clouds to imagine shapes so we used the leaves and branches instead.

'The veins and bruises on Dad's legs after he's been playing soccer.'

'Um, Lucy's hair in that stupid ponytail that she puts on top of her head when we play netball.'

'A sick brain.'

'Ooh, good one. Fairy floss.'

'Which makes me think ... do you have any money?' Angus asked. 'We could go to the shops.'

'I don't think they sell fairy floss.' I laughed.

'No, but they have my favourite liquorice.'

I chose a python jube and Angus bought hard liquorice squares.

'Want to walk to the creek?' Angus asked.

The creek, when it had any water, trickled next to the teachers' college and then pooled behind a house and beside a park. Students would cut class and go there to smoke. There were lots of butts lying around and mosquitoes hovered above the still water. We sat on a large, flat rock, shielded by overhanging branches.

'Did you know a mosquito can lay three hundred eggs at a time?' Angus asked.

'No, but I'm not surprised.'

'It's about the same number of freckles you have on your legs.'

'Have you counted them?'

'I tried to during one of Mr Temple's history classes, you know, the ones where he drones on through whole chapters. You have 154 on your left leg and 146 on your right.'

Angus moved closer. His peach-soft skin made him look younger, which is why he grew his sandy-brown hair long and shaggy.

'I like hanging out with you, Celia.'

He kissed me softly at first, then pushing harder with his warm lips. I worried whether to put my tongue in his mouth or not. And if I put it in, did I move it around? I could remember Penny talking about kissing a guy whose tongue felt like a huge slug. I decided to copy whatever Angus did. He tasted like aniseed.

'Have you kissed anyone before?' he asked.

'No.'

I had kissed Peter Lassiter at last year's school dance. Forced into it by my friend Julie, who was a year older. 'Go on, Celia, kiss Peter', she urged me. In the dim lighting of the dance hall balcony, Peter and I moved awkwardly towards each other. His mouth was over mine, dribbly and cold and tasting of rum.

'Neither have I', said Angus. 'Want to do it again?' He grinned.

In the weeks that followed I replayed our kisses in my head over and over again. I saved all the text messages he sent until my phone was full. I had to force myself to concentrate in class.

Through all this I sensed that something at home had changed, but I was too absorbed with Angus to take much notice. Dad talked quietly to Mum all the time. Rather than ask what was going on, I would instead think about what I might say to Angus in my next text or email.

Jeremy often came to our house to cook dinner. I imagined Angus at his home with Kathleen, eating by themselves. Jeremy made beef bourguignon one night. He explained to Mum that she had to cut out the tiny green hearts of a garlic clove because they were bitter. Mum licked her lips. I couldn't understand how she liked the bourguignon because it was thick with mushrooms, which she hated. To me it was stew.

Dad and Jeremy got along okay at these dinners. I don't think Dad knew Jeremy was the cook most of the time. Dad always arrived late, having dumped his fishy overalls or dusty clothes in the laundry.

One night Jeremy helped Dad gut the fishes brought back

from Uncle George's. They crouched down by the side of our house near the tap and scraped scales onto a sheet of plastic. Then they sliced the fishes' bellies. Dad hooked the entrails with his chunky fingers. Jeremy flicked the guts with the blunt side of a knife. I lay on the wooden seat and watched.

'Kathleen mind you being out all the time?' Dad asked.

'She gets headaches. We'd go mad if we stayed home with her; all the tiptoeing around.'

'Yeah, well, for me, I like to be out of the house, too—really out, like on a boat, or up a tree, or in the forest.'

I thought Dad and Jeremy were similar in a way. They both had inquiring minds. It's just that Jeremy's took him to books and Dad's had taken him to finding out how things worked with his hands. Dad had made our cubbyhouse from bits of wood, and he patched holes in our canoes.

One day Dad was lopping a tree in our garden—tossing the branches like knitting needles—when a large branch crushed Mum's favourite rosebushes. Two bushes she had grown and pruned so that they perfectly shielded our lounge room from people walking past on the street. I found her crying in the shed. I hugged her and told her I was sorry about that branch and those bushes. She told me that I was too young to have been able to see what had happened.

It took me awhile to work out that she hadn't been talking about trees and bushes at all; that she'd actually been crying over Penny. It turned out that the huddled conversations I'd seen between Mum and Dad had been desperate worrying and simmering rage because Penny had involved herself in a serious relationship during her important years at school. They eventually found out Penny had chosen to date a man twice her age and that man was Jeremy. A *married* man. Our gallant protector.

My mother said later that she could see my sister's youth and happiness wither and disappear. I think Mum also felt guilty. All those rules to keep Penny close to home so her grades wouldn't be affected and Mum had unwittingly allowed the greatest distraction to flourish under our noses. I was too caught up in Angus, and Mum, well; I guess she felt flattered at Jeremy's attention, not knowing it was really directed elsewhere.

I was in my bedroom removing my toenail polish, using a tiny cotton bud to soak up the remaining drips of nail polish remover, when I heard Dad shouting.

'Come in this house and I'll kill you! We've had Kathleen's bloody sisters around here, mate. You've got a mess at home. I'd cut your losses.'

I heard Penny's voice in the distance.

Glass shattered and there was a dull thump. The house trembled.

I thought a bird had flown into my bedroom window; it sounded so close. But it was too late for birds.

Then I heard Mum: 'Oh no, no'.

My chest was icy. Then my bedroom door was pulled firmly closed.

'Don't come out, Celia', Dad said.

*

Afterwards, Dad went to live in one of Uncle George's cabins in the bush. Jeremy didn't visit anymore. Penny ended up with a scar under her chin. I know she still talked to Jeremy, though, because I saw his name in her email inbox. Somehow I think if Dad hadn't lost his temper that night his position in our family may have been restored. But by lunging at another man in the kitchen and inadvertently sending your daughter flying into an open cupboard, it seemed that his ability to protect us was further compromised.

Mum was finally angry. It was apparent in the agitated way she cleaned out cupboards and hacked at overgrown bushes. She spoke harshly to Penny. I felt nauseous and tense, like there were lots of things I needed to think about but none that I wanted to.

Angus moved schools. Then his family moved out of town altogether. I felt like he blamed Penny. And because she was my sister, I felt like he also blamed me.

I wasn't supposed to visit Dad at his cabin. He worked less now and he looked weary. We never talked about that night. All I knew for sure was that Mum wasn't ready to forgive him, or Jeremy, or Penny.

Whenever I walked along the wide tyre tracks towards Dad's riverside cabin, I thought of Angus and our kiss at the creek. I wondered if Angus thought of me.

The worn away grass reminded me of the bare carpet next to Mum's bed where she put her feet everyday. Would Dad be in the cabin long enough to wear out a patch on the rug next to his bed?

Dad's cabin sat on the flat right next to the olive-green river mouth. One day we sat on his cabin steps. His energy and temper seemed to have been sucked into the dark sky. Even his hands seemed smaller.

'How's school going?'

'Good. All As and Bs this term.'

I watched a rainbow appear.

'Knowledge is a good thing, Celia, but it needs to be

coupled with practical things. There are laws of nature and laws of people. You might not agree with them, but they're there for a reason.'

I thought of Angus and the three hundred eggs that mosquitoes lay. I didn't understand.

'Sometimes you can't have what you want', Dad said.

'Can you come home?'

He snapped a twig in his hand.

'I'd like to, Celia.'

As I walked home that night the breeze crept around my legs. What if that dolphin had been a shark? Would there always have been something that brought the tide in over my family?

Poets Don't Do Gym

Isabel Robinson

On the street a boy
as cropped and chiselled
as a marble god
tempts me with
free sessions
at some temple of the body.
But I am a poet
and poets don't do gym.

Those black suit saviours
peddling salvation.
Flat wraparound eyes
mirror my shapeless hide
and prick me with the
balloon of guilt.

Didn't I say already
that poets don't do gym?

Listen sonny,
poets do wine and beer.
They do whisky and gin
and brandy and kerosene
while fighting pink dragons.
They smoke filters and rollies,
the pipe, the joint, the cigarillo.
They cough up words.

They do madness
and poverty,
the needle,
the speed pill,
the white powder.
They can't pay the rent
or feed their children.
Verses scuttle away like roaches.

They take the gas pipe
and the train track.
The rope's caress, the razor's bite.
From the stern of a boat
they tango with their muse
in that dark, blue dive.
Need I say it again?
Poets don't do gym.

The Shady Side: Her Life in Taipei

Nadeemy Chen

Excerpts from 'The Shady Side: Her Life in Taipei'

MISS CANADA AND THE KILLER ROACHES

Share housing in Taipei often means living with a plague of flying killer roaches. Killer roaches are no bigger than the ones we have in Australia—they just have more charisma. They're squat-dwelling anarchists who hide out in the walls and chortle about the hysteria that always accompanies their timely raids.

In Taipei I bore witness to the most rampant, panic-stricken horror brought about by these diminutive shuttling creatures. Aside from Taipei's city slickers who fear everything not made of plastic, Canadians and Europeans seemed particularly petrified by these monstrous, tropical manifestations. So petrified, in fact, that before moving into one apartment I was adamantly warned to never open the balcony door. Behind it, I was told, lay a hovel of breeding roaches awaiting any opportunity to invade human territory and infect it with a range of vile diseases.

I moved in despite the warning and, after a confounding spell of share housing, became quite accustomed to my Canadian roomie's habit of clapping rapidly and whistling at the doorway of each room before entering. This was done, she said, to 'scare' the roaches into hiding and avoid any nasty confrontations. Despite her defence strategies, one roach found its way into her piles of sweaty socks and underwear and lay in waiting.

That particular roach was bent on tormenting her and the highlight round came late one night. The roach shuttled back and forth across her room, before running at her in a fully fledged kung-fu style attack. It then gloatingly crawled all over her bed, before using it as a runway to fly into her hair. During these ten minutes of terror Miss Canada slipped into the fits of an anxiety attack, enhanced by wide-mouthed screams and hyperventilating. It was a mad show, but the timing drove me to pull myself out of bed and genteelly release the roach into the night.

Miss Canada's neurosis was nothing special, though. In that apartment alone, there was Miss Poland, Miss Switzerland and Miss Japan and they all suffered horrible abuse from roaches on the loose. After salvaging several more nasty situations, I was finally crowned The Cockroach Queen—a true saviour for my courteous and unfailing dedication to roach removal. I even began to crave the ear-splitting cries of my name, followed by the sporadic screams and general hysteria. They came at unexpected times, from unexpected corners of the house, and continued until the offender had been expelled. Miss Japan even took to the couch for a week once after being unable to apprehend a very suspect intruder—a master in the art of shape-shifting—who insisted on disappearing and reappearing in her room.

As one would expect, I had a number of male competitors for roach-saviour status. I tried to ward them off, exercising only the cleanest and most humane methods of removal, but I eventually lost out. I guess I will never be 'man enough' to flex my biceps and then shoot at a roach for ten minutes with a handheld firecracker!

***

CANADIAN PSYCHO

Only locals know that eighty per cent of the expat community in Taipei is Canadian. There is about one Canadian for every roach in the city and, considering the levels of this infestation, it's impossible not to meet them. They're everywhere. On every street corner, in every bar and every restaurant, on the MRT, in the bus—and they're always yelling 'Fuckin' A' or being revoltingly encouraging. I was taking off my shoes at the door once, when my Canadian manager breezed past with a 'You're doing a *great* job, there!'

Despite their general goodwill, I had the novel experience of share housing with the original Canadian Psycho (CP). The thing about a real psychopath is that they look normal: they dress in civvies, go to work like everyone else and leave chocolate bunny-faced croissants outside your bedroom.

At first CP was a fairly quiet roommate who tried to keep his long, unrequited love for Miss Canada out of sight. The first release from his tormented bondage came just before my arrival on the scene. He had shacked up with her cousin, had his first man-on-man experience, and then driven his lover out of town with a tornado of father issues. Following his lover's quick departure, CP went to India and 'found himself' then fell into rampant denial about his homosexuality, stalwartly insisting he could never fall in love with a man and would never engage in the 'disgusting practices' of anal sex. Nonetheless, drunken nights always ended up with Chinese boys on his cock and the empty threat that he was going to urinate on my face. These events were inevitably followed by seventeen-page letters of tearful abuse directed at Miss Canada, accusing her of being a cold, heartless, soulless bitch-skank who fucked up every relationship in *her* life. Not forgetting he was Canadian, however, he still courteously greeted us whenever he came home, before running to his room and slamming his door.

At this point let me mention that I had a total of three extended conversations with CP during our four months of share housing. But in his mind I became part of the axis of evil: a fucked-up bitch and a sidekick to Miss Canada's cruel torment. I first realised this when CP put his single birthday card out on display. It read: *HAPPY BIRTHDAY, SORRY YOUR ROOMIES ARE SUCH HOES*! Soon after, CP convinced himself I was involved in espionage and sabotage and ascertained that I was a mindless puppet under the directions of Miss Canada. Paranoid schizophrenics, eat your hearts out! It all began to climax around the time I made arrangements to move apartments. I sent CP an SMS to make a time to tie up our apartment's odds and ends, and was met by three days of silence then an onslaught of wild accusations. All I could think was, 'CP, I just want to talk about the bills'.

In the final days, and to guarantee complications as the psychotic do, CP sequestered most of the furniture and hid it in his locked room. I know this because, feeling I had restrained my cuckoo's-nest alter ego for too long, I broke into his room and returned the stolen wares to their rightful places. He responded by throwing rice all over the apartment, re-sequestering the TV and leaving me a note that said: *Knowing you has taught me a whole new level of immaturity—good luck with getting a mind of your own.* I should have left it, but the cuckoo was out. I re-re-sequestered the TV and left him a page-long letter that concluded: *Crawl into a fucking hole and die. Oh, and if I ever see you again, I'll have you knifed.*

CP's new roommates arrived home first that day and found my note. Bear in mind that what I have exposed was just the endnotes to a much longer piece. At first the new English tenants thought the entire letter was for them. They called me in teary distress: 'Um, we found your letter, yeah. Well, um, it wasn't very nice. You didn't mean it, right? It was just a joke, yeah? You don't really want us to give it to him, do you?'

I guess they finally decided to give my letter to CP because on the day he left Taipei a series of ads appeared in the personal columns on Tealit.com, a site frequented by Taipei's expats. They all bore my name and number or Miss Canada's name and number. Some claimed we were *young girls looking for fun with both foreign and Chinese men* and others claimed we were *seeking new roommates*. My first call came through from Dubai at three o'clock in the morning—a soon-to-arrive businessman had seen my Arabic name and was looking for a wife. Miss Canada and I received close to a hundred phone calls that week. Everything from men wanting sex, to language-exchange prospects, to new roomies. *Viva la vida*!

***

THE SEVEN SOCIALLY IMPOVERISHED DWARFS

Like every expat community, Taipei's expats come in posses. You can round them up and slot them snugly into boxes: students, adventurers, escapists, vagabonds, ageing hippies, embassy whores, etc., etc. Unfortunately for Taipei there are also a disproportionate number of dropkicks and social misfits on the loose. Most of them are ageing men, flying high on the greatest ego-tripping roller-coaster orgies of their lifetimes. The bitter, foreign women have fled, but the Taiwanese have to stay. In my workplace alone, I was the only foreign woman with seven foreign men and at the tender age of twenty-six was the youngest staff member by a good five years.

And so began the heart-rending tale of *Snow Yellow and the Seven Socially Impoverished Dwarfs*. There was Dopey, Sticky, Gloomy, Drippy, Choppy, Dribbly and Lazy-Eye. Dopey was too stoned to know he was a teacher, Sticky liked to talk about his wet dreams, Gloomy suffered from world domination delusions, Drippy had no availing personality, Choppy was the all-star American kung-fu hero, Dribbly kindly only talked about my breasts when he was drunk and Lazy-Eye was the manager who saw nothing that went on. But he wasn't the dwarf-leader. The little-man leader was Sticky, who came crowned with a history of sexual harassment in the workplace and a best friend who even made it onto national television for assaulting a girl in a nightclub. Since getting hitched, Sticky has tried to repair his ways and no longer touches female staff members—at least not when others are looking.

Over the year, Sticky and I had some pretty, well, 'sticky' encounters. There was the time in gym class I told him his smutty puppy dog eyes weren't cute at all and he told me there was nothing I could do about it because I wasn't in my nice, cushy, rights-respecting country anymore. There was also the time when he wandered into my classroom to openly share his fantasies of me feeling up other girls in public bathhouses. And then there was the last time we spoke. Sticky sauntered into my classroom and, with his eyes on my tits, announced to my class that I was the most arrogant person he had ever met. After school I let loose on Sticky with a heated '–isms' lecture: sexism, professionalism, etc. and topped it all off with a few warnings and low-aimed insults.

Over the next six months Sticky and I didn't exchange a word, but he did send some of the dwarf-henchmen to chat with me. Silly little Snow Yellow; so little did I know and how much they have taught me. I now know that: mothers who enter the school building are asking to be eyeballed; secretarial staff should feel privileged if married dwarfs 'choose' them for infidelity; commenting on the size of a woman's tits in the workplace is a compliment; sexual harassment is better than physical violence (and apparently I have to choose one); and mentioning your wet dreams in front of a class of ten year olds is A-okay.

***

PENGHU: UGLY ISLAND

Taiwan is not a haven for backpackers or happy campers and Taiwan's *Lonely Planet* was clearly written in absentia. The only guarantee is that if it is written in *Lonely Planet Taiwan* it is either long gone, only part of the story, or a wild, unsubstantiated claim. In a slow and painful way I have learnt that spontaneity only reaps trouble and travel in Taiwan requires careful planning, hotel or tour bookings and scooter rental in advance.

On my final, untoward adventure, I dragged my menopausal mother to the Penghu Islands in the Taiwan Strait. *Lonely Planet Taiwan (2004)* claims that Penghu is 'a popular summertime destination for its white sandy beaches, swimming, camping, windsurfing and beautiful coral beaches' and 'a trip through history, with its preserved fishing villages and beautiful temples'. Other claims are that the islands have a beautiful, windswept landscape which contrasts with Taiwan's mountainous tropics.

After a four-day sentence, my mother and I have renamed Penghu 'Ugly Island'. This is primarily for its barren landscape of debris and trash, but also for its devastating lack of trees and geographical contrast. In short, it is flat, empty and covered in mutilated pine tree stumps. Contrary to *Lonely Planet*'s claims that camping is permitted, Penghu is a strategic and contentious military base located between mainland Taiwan and China and active military training programs mean no beach access.

My mother and I spent our first night in a tiled, windowless room animated by the whine of mosquitoes and the whitish glow of a single fluorescent bulb. To escape the impending claustrophobia we ventured to the annual fireworks festival, or Mother's Day Variety Show, with its jostling crowd of 30,000. This was a great holiday opener for my Aussie mother, who sees Mother's Day as a day for everyone else to piss off and give her some long-deserved peace. The event was made even more chaotic by the appearance of a local god, who manifested suddenly in glowing fibreglass offset by flashing blue-diamond bonsai. The green laser beam coming out of his third eye lit up a crowd awed by the fire shooting out of his hands. Then, as we broke past the worshippers, we found ourselves privy to wannabe rockstars, school choirs, karaoke-style ballads and crackling fireworks—all which paled under the spectacle of a giant neon rainbow that sent a reflective shimmer across the river. I soon realised, however, that the god was not the only sideshow. I snapped out of my neon-reverie to find myself surrounded by TV cameras, dazzling lights and a reporter shooting questions at me in Chinese. Luckily, my mother was in good Leo-form. She pushed me aside and, with no qualms about being understood, gave a complete rundown of the night in English and made it onto National Taiwan News.

The next day we left the cheap hotels of Penghu for the nearby island of Chipei. Arrival brought the vision of a true nuclear landscape: flattened plains of landfills and dust, intense winds, scorching heat, heavy smog, few surviving plants or buildings and a coastline littered with the debris of destroyed tombs. (I later found out that the tomb-smashing was intentional, as after drying out the bones of the ancestors they are returned to the family home.) Forget about campgrounds with running water, beach-front cafes, swinging hammocks, tropical cocktails and ripples licking golden sand. Chipei meant camping alone in a small, solitary patch of pine trees and rubbish, with severe sunstroke and headaches, violent sandstorms and shores littered with twisting sea snakes.

We were facing three days of utter abjection: no books, no games, no music and no extended company. My mother began by blaming me for the geographical deficiencies and lack of 'Keep Penghu Beautiful' campaigns. She informed me I had some 'hare-brained ideas', partnered by the more vehement 'when you reach my age, you are going to regret the suffering you put me through'. To ensure her prophecy comes true I made her ride on the back of a 100 cc scooter, strung in handbags, travel packs, sleeping bags, a four-man tent and a mattress. The lowest points, however, were our mealtime tensions. Chipei is incredibly remote and survives primarily on a staple of rice and fish—my mother is allergic to both—and my Chinese is not particularly advanced. Somehow we ended up on a diet of giant snails and sea urchin pancakes, which I have discovered to be the most effective laxatives after magic mushrooms. Great for camping without a trowel, without toilet paper and without bathrooms or running water for miles!

Sunshine

Victoria Brookman

The girl with the parasol scowled. It had been three days. Three days since she had decided to spoil the world. If she couldn't have it, no one would.

And yet, the whole world was at once too fulfilled with a gush of sweet warmth that left no hour for discontent. The sun shone and the birds tweeted. Cars drove past on the street and the sky was a faultless blue. Hammers could be heard down the street and people walked past, talking amongst themselves.

An aeroplane flew casually overhead. She picked her nose in frustration. *Could this have been a stupid idea?*

Peering down the driveway, she saw a fragile snail spreading a gooey, sparkly trail down the pavers. *Fuck my life*, she thought. *Fuck you all to hell. I could crush you right now, snail.*

A rush of power flushed through her skin. Hairs stood on end. She could destroy its world right now—that would be a start. She started towards the snail. The dog over the road barked crazily at nothing, as usual. She stopped and peered through the warm sunlight. The snail had picked up pace and was making its way to a wall for shelter.

*

She woke from her slumber at approximately one-oh-three. She sat bolt upright. She'd already failed twice this morning. No job to go to, she'd not only slept for half the day but she'd missed her doctor's appointment. She'd have to wait 'til Tuesday to get the swine flu shot, now.

Fuck, fuck, fuck, fuck, she ranted, threw on her scraggy dressing-gown and ran to the kitchen to put on her toast. Outside, her retarded housemate stood in the driveway peering around herself in the sunlight with her parasol in hand.

Shaking her head, she flicked on the TV to Sky News and then squeezed some lemon juice into a cup of tap water. She pondered the taste of plain water now that the desalination plant had opened. The Eastern Suburbs were supposed to get the new water from the sea, which reportedly tasted weird. All plain water tasted weird if you'd been flavouring it with lemon juice for long enough.

She sat down with her plate of veggie-and-cheese toast, probiotic capsule, multivitamin and Sky News. She hoped both that her housemate would stay on the driveway and that the idiot box would provide an update on the latest debacles in state politics. Or another thing to laugh at about Tony

Abbott would suffice. She was sorely disappointed yet again. *Ahh, random CBS broadcast in place of local news, that's what we pay the Foxtel bills for …*

*

Her attention was momentarily stolen away from the confusing path to the destruction of all life by unexpected, loud American accents coming from the living room. Her heart skipped a beat. *What the hell is that?* She stood there, paralysed by the thought that her house really was haunted. Trying to block it out, she looked up at the patterns on her parasol and spun it around so that the colours darted through the blue of the sky. It was hot and humid. Simply perfect. Someone dutifully practiced scales on a clarinet down the street.

Maybe she should reconsider this whole 'destroy the world' thing. It occurred to her that if she did manage to destroy it, there would be no mechanism by which to enjoy her triumph. Maybe this was why evil as a practice had never really taken hold; why there were no riots in the street, just the chant of cicadas and the hum of the buses meandering up the hill.

*

Sick of gubernatorial scandals, she jumped up and sorted an 'essential' pile of dirty washing to throw in the machine. She carefully sprayed stain remover on dirty collars of business shirts and food splatters from the creation of last night's chicken tikka. Throwing the stain booster in, followed by the normal laundry powder, she felt like a witch over a frothing cauldron.

Bubble, bubble, toil and trouble ... She pushed the buttons: eco, cold, start. God, she was good. Stepping back from the gushing machine, she pondered her situation: 'feminist housewife'. She'd never thought she might spend time doing the household chores and cooking while hubby was out earning the rent, but suddenly without a job that was her life. She wiped some sweat from her brow with the back of her hand, brushing her fringe off her face. Her inner teenager could whinge all she liked, but living in a pigsty was not a form of feminist direct action.

*

The sun sizzled the tops of her feet, drawing her attention away and momentarily distracting her from her thoughts of quickening snails, Americans and world detonation. But curiosity was getting the better of her: she had to find out why there were Americans blaring in her living room. Had they hopped over the back fence? Had they sensed her weakening resolve to destroy the world and decided to take her place? Were they planning a pep talk? A logical voice in her mind shouted, *You idiot! You're just a twenty-something girl from Bondi. Why would the world care what you think? The voices are from the—*

Clouds of anger brewed inside her again. She felt them mounting up beneath her diaphragm. That was the point, wasn't it? That no one cared? She knew how she thought suicide bombers must feel before they move to detonate. Utter despair and powerlessness, the only solution being a small window through which you must crawl to make your point. She lowered her parasol and peered in the doorway.

*

She drummed her fingers on the top of the washing machine, which slowly began to hum. Slow, rhythmic, full of purpose. She realised that she kind of enjoyed the simplicity of home life. It wasn't like she was restricted because of her gender; she could go get a job anytime she wanted. The only thing she needed to work on was waking up before noon. Even waking up *at* noon would be a start.

What to do next? It was too early for lunch. Maybe apply some sunscreen and read outside? That might be nice. She had a lot of reading to do.

Sun protection is *important*. She thought of her housemate's dainty parasol: *they're definitely coming back into fashion, no thanks to weirdos like—*

*

She gasped. Her eyes were adjusting from being in the sunlight for too long, but she was sure there was no one in the room. The voices continued. Slowly her vision returned and she realised they were coming through a speaker. Healthcare reform, Iran. She spun around and saw the TV on full blare. It had sounded so real. It was a shame, really. She'd already come up with a draft set of questions and statements for the Americans. But they weren't really talking to her; they were talking to each other. Loneliness reinstated itself.

*

Weirdos were the main problems in her life at the moment. She sighed, wandered inside to the kitchen and stopped for a moment. *If I could just separate myself from anyone with an IQ under 130, anyone with any kind of strange, socially awkward obsessions and anyone who believes in superstitions like the tooth fairy and 'God' ...*

Silently searching through the cupboards for any kind of vaguely healthy snack, she found a bunch of bananas tucked away. Fruit flies circled ominously nearby. She supposed it would be another productive action she could tick off today—eating food before it goes bad.

*

Her heart pounded with rage once more. Didn't anyone want to interact with her? Even a snail, for fuck's sake, defied logic to avoid her. She felt like an empty shell, exactly as she supposed society thought she existed. Destruction or construction? Words tortured her. She knew how to end her dilemma once and for all.

*

She searched around in the drawer for a suitable knife to cut the banana into small pieces to plop into yoghurt. *Is this even healthy?* She wondered, *should I cut through the skin or remove it first?* She reached for the big knife. *I can't believe this is what I'm pondering these days. I could scream my fucking head off.*

*

This'll teach the world to leave me sad and lonely, head filled with crazy thoughts all day. She tripped on a laundry basket. The pain from her stubbed toe would be irrelevant soon.

*

She wandered out to the backyard to double-check that the washing machine was on 'cold', knife still in hand. She heard someone rustling through the drawers in the kitchen. She dreaded the mundane nature of the conversation with her housemate which would inevitably follow. *Could one person be more boring?*

*

She appeared in the kitchen, certain she'd heard someone again. She dismissed more crazy thoughts, despite the open back door.
    The universe continued to conspire against her. *Where the hell is the good, big, sharp knife?* Frustrated, she stormed into the bathroom and turned the bath taps on full bore.

*

She felt a bit bad that she was so mean to her boring, nut case housemate. A girl with a parasol was clearly crying out for attention. Maybe she just needed some normality? Maybe they could swap? She wandered in, put the knife in the kitchen and walked outside again into the blinding sunlight. *Hmm, parasols …*

*

Water pounded on water as the rickety old pipes shook with the force of her final bath. *I'll slit my wrists alone in the bath. I'll be dead and undiscovered for days. I'll show you all!*

*

She needed some meaning outside this domestic framework. Something—anything—interesting must occur. Even just something weird would be fine. Examining the sky, she cradled cut-up banana in her hands and listened to the nearby crashing waves.

*

She darted back into the scabby kitchen and picked up a dirty knife that seemed to have appeared on the edge of the kitchen sink. She briefly considered the hygiene aspects. It looked a bit like banana.

*

She sighed, turning from the outside world and back to the realities of domesticity. It was time to go inside and mate the banana with its yoghurt. Maybe see what the nut case was up to. It would ward off boredom for the next five minutes.

*

Still in the kitchen, she thought she might cut herself here, now. *A trail of blood; how melodramatic.*

*

Wandering into the shared space of domestic bliss that was the kitchen, she was shocked to see her boring, nut case housemate in a state of action.

*

She stood, eyes frantic with desperate loneliness, knife at the ready on her wrist. Driven crazy by the thought that she was crazy, her mind ticked over.

*

She stood, mind awakening with startled curiosity, mouth ready to say anything that came to mind.
    'Having a bath, are you?'

New Bones

Amy Brown

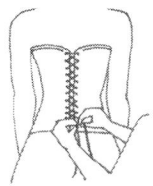

I bought new bones
because the ones I had were bent and bowed.
I bought new bones
because the ones I had were frail,
chalky and afraid.

Lace me. Bind me.
Cinch me in and thrust me out.
Draw me, tie me,
splay me on the floor.
Dress me up and strip me down:
you cannot bend me anymore.

I bought new bones
when the ones I had were only human.

I bought new bones:
they bear me up in satin and steel;

you cannot bend me anymore.

Panda
Amy German

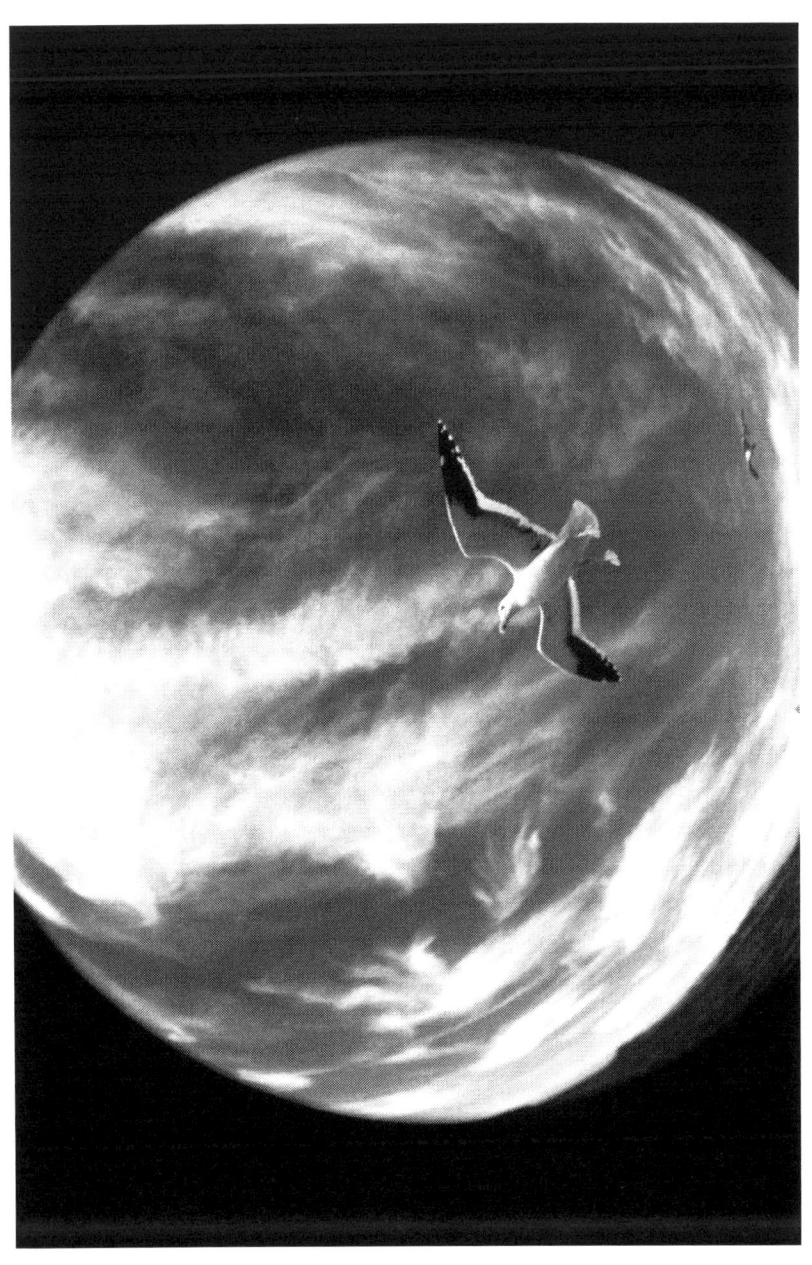

Seagull
Amy German

Fourteen

Katie Henderson-Brooks

I abandoned ship at fourteen.
And I felt, and I felt and I felt
As I battered back the waves
Within.

Air forced its way into my lungs.

My daughter remarked that my birth was Venus-themed;
I begged to differ: my naissance was wrought by Jonah.
Sunk, swallowed, spat.

Air forced its way into my lungs.
And I had no white whale to distract me so I
Felt and I felt and I felt.

Years and months and hours existed but meant nothing—
Time was etched into my skin by the salt of the storms.
My husband remarked that my death was an homage to Lazarus:
But I am more than man; I'm cat—
I have more lives than that.

Yes, dear, I abandoned ship at fourteen.
I left others at the helm,
I let the anchor rust right through.

And yet air forced its way into my lungs,
So I feel, and I feel and I feel.

The Start

Connie Theresa Ye

The doctor cannot meet her eye. Inside her brain is screaming for release.

'I'm afraid so. The results came back positive.'

He is afraid. And if he is afraid, what is she to be?

Instinctively her parents reach out for her hands. They hold each other in the silence while the doctor outlines the disease. Her hands feel cold; she has roaring static between her ears from the blood throughout her entire body convening and rushing towards her head.

*

On the way to school the girl on the bus beside her is incredibly heavy-set and sensuous, swaying in rhythm with every jolt and speed bump. Her expression, too, is serene and unworried. She could be one of those Venetian Renaissance women sitting for a portrait: deliciously poised and self-assured in her comfortable bulk. Drawing her shirt more closely around her, hoping fervently that her neighbour will not notice with disgust the hollows in her collarbone and the sharp helicopter blades of her shoulders.

But during the day she forgets. Like when the pipe to their front-loading washing machine bursts yet again and she hears her mother swear exasperatedly. She has to help her mother wrench open the glass door with grey water swirling around her ankles along with her unwashed underwear. She can still laugh at that absurd teamwork, the cold seeping through her knees as she tries to block the relentless gush of water with her bare hands which after a while feel numb.

There are times like those when she forgets that the emaciated, pockmarked limbs are her own. That the trembling, jaundiced fingers which threaten to surrender everyday objects to gravity are still controlled by her own brain, connecting and firing neurons which seem as remote from her failing, faltering heart as a robot is from flesh.

Positive. Positive. She lies awake in bed at night, rolling the word over her tongue. It ticks like a broken, dripping tap in the back of her head. The door to her room is left ajar and from across the dim corridor she can hear the creaking bedsprings of her parents' equally sleepless nights. She can tell from the uneven breathing that they, too, are kept awake by dripping taps in the backs of their heads. She draws comfort from the sound of her parents' broken, unintelligible murmurs, their attempts to console each other, their useless comments on daily events. The whisperings and rumblings carry over across the corridor and envelop her in a bittersweet blanket. The three of them lie awake at night, held together by this fierce, helpless strength.

*

She is too young for this decaying body. After all these years of cohabitation, the once-mutual agreement and support her mind provided for her body and vice versa has deteriorated into a cold war. An embargo of sorts placed upon her heart, her liver. With the age-old treaties torn to shreds, her mind prepares for an assault of depression to which her body responds by simply shutting down. With little skirmishes here and there the pockets of resistance break out on her neck and face. These battle scars send her stumbling back to base camp—even the mirror recoils as she blinks back tears while the nurse gently and ineffectively dabs the ointment on her weeping skin.

And she, the helpless onlooker, watches these retaliations hurled back and forth, lurching in and out of consciousness.

For three weeks she has lain in this cot. She has become a child once more; her parents peering in anxiously over the railings, watching and guarding her last tottering steps as they once oversaw her first. She commits herself the tug and pull. Like a swimmer who has been clinging to the rocky outcrops for far too long and, tired from the constant battering of waves, allows oneself to be swept away out to sea. That was what she meant when she wanted to go home, they said.

Her mother looks on helpless as her father wanders through the house, lost and cut adrift. The rooms all look strangely the same; unfamiliar with their white, bare, sterile walls. Her room looks exactly the same, the pillows neat as if she were simply staying over at a friends' place.

People come to take away the oxygen tanks, the drip stand, the unfinished medication. Her father sits among them on her bed, bewildered with their quiet efficiency. They leave in the same unobtrusive manner and her mother appears in the doorway, the burden lifted from her face.

They surface on dry land together, gasping at the raw air where the terrain is familiar yet unfamiliar and the wind blows a strange new smell. It is the strangest start.

Countdown to an Emigration

James Nathaniel-Grant

Excerpts from 'Sunburnt: A New Life in Australia'

T MINUS ONE WEEK: SEPARATION

'At least your grandfather doesn't think you're gay anymore', said Meg, placing her hand on my knee in a vain gesture of reassurance.

'I don't think that's going to be any consolation for him, Meg. He never seemed that fussed about whether I was straight or not. He just wanted me to be happy and to see me more often', I replied, before pausing.

'And now you're worried you'll never see him again', said my wife, articulating a possibility I was trying hard not to accept.

Meg and I were driving away from our last visit to my oldest living relative. Grandad had always been rather good about what he had assumed was my sexuality. He had grown up part of an intolerant generation whose members would not readily have admitted in public to having a homosexual grandson. But despite this, and notwithstanding his considerable age, he never once asked me potentially awkward questions when I failed yet again to bring home an attractive girl to meet him. I would turn up at his Lincolnshire home alone once more, we would talk about his gardening and he would politely refrain from asking why I didn't have a girlfriend. He would tell me about the latest local tournament at the lawn bowls club in Cherry Willingham and he would never betray his disappointment at the unlikelihood of my ever getting married and having kids.

But now that he realised that my years of solitude had been more a function of consistent bad luck and ineptitude with girls than a preference for other men, he had been dealt a blow he could never have expected: the woman of my dreams was an antipodean.

When he first clapped eyes on Meg his jaw temporarily dislocated itself from the rest of his face before bouncing off the kitchen tiles to resettle a more respectable distance below his eternally rigid upper lip. Mouth still ajar, he stumbled to greet her, shook her hand politely and then needed to sit down promptly. I gathered a couple of wine glasses while my grandfather did the same with his thoughts. It was a response uncannily similar to mine when I had first seen Meg, sitting behind a table at a *pizzeria* in Rome in the autumn of 2001. But with his ninety-four years and the shock of seeing me with a female flaxen-haired beauty, his excuse was better than any available to me three years previously.

Before I met Meg the prospect of emigrating for a stunning blonde bureaucrat with a foreign affairs career in Australia had never figured anywhere in my dreams, let alone my future life intentions. But I found myself, after an hour of excited conversation, breaking the news to my grandfather that I was following Meg back to her homeland. She had become increasingly homesick and had raised the possibility of our starting anew in an exotic country 10,000 miles away. She had presented it in her typically compelling manner: I could either stay alone drinking warm, flat beer in the unremitting rain of south-east England or I could accompany her to a land dotted with kangaroos, drenched in sun and fringed with white sand. It was likely celibacy in cold Surrey versus guaranteed hot sex in Sydney. It had been a difficult choice—for the fleeting moment it took me to make a decision that would irrevocably change our lives.

A couple of months later, while Meg popped out tactfully to give us some time alone, my grandfather wished me all the best. But he would only let me leave on one condition.

'I want to know all about what happens in Australia, James. Why don't you write me a letter every so often?'

'I don't know, Grandad. I'm not much of a writer.'

'You're anything you want to be and don't you forget that. Who knows, you might find that moving to a new country makes you want to write in a way you've never wanted to before', my grandfather said, with a worldly look in his eyes that hinted of secret knowledge from a past of which I knew little.

My father had told me that Grandad had been sent to Ontario as a boy to work as a labourer for his uncle on a vast cattle farm in the bleak central plains of Canada. I knew that he had run away aged seventeen to join the Royal Navy as the only route by which he thought he might eventually be able to return to his native England. But he never talked of his harsh upbringing nor the conflict and suffering that he saw during World War II.

'I'm not so sure, but I'll write you a postcard if we go on holiday', I said, hesitantly.

'How about you just write a diary? I wish I'd kept the one I wrote when I was your age.'

By late afternoon time was getting on; over the next few days I had to organise the transportation of my entire life to Australia. So I reluctantly explained we had to go. Outside the back door to his small farmhouse, my grandfather turned his head away so that I couldn't see his face. He mumbled something that sounded like:

'I fear this will be the last ... that I won't ... that we won't ...'

'We'll be back on holiday, don't worry. We'll see you again soon, Grandad. Probably next year or the year after', I said, trying to soothe both his and my fears.

But deep down I knew that there was, of course, the possibility that we would not be back so soon. That we would not, in fact, see him again. That this would be the final farewell.

When my grandfather turned his head back to face me his eyes were glistening with an unnatural sheen. The reflective lustre of stifled tears took me aback—I hadn't expected this. But I carried on smiling and looking cheerful as I shook his hand, refusing to give him any indication that it had even crossed my mind that this might be our last handshake.

'Even if I don't see you again I still want to hear what you're up to, young man', he said.

'Of course we'll see each other again', I replied. 'But don't worry, Grandad. I'll keep a diary in any event and I'll phone to tell you the best stories. I promise.'

Meg gave my grandfather a brief hug and he perked up, saying how lovely it had been to meet her. Then Meg took my arm and subtly led me towards the car. I got in on the passenger side, Meg started the engine and we moved off, tyres crunching along the gravel drive. We drove towards moss-covered timber gates, beyond which the tapering line of a narrow lane led away from my grandfather's house to wend its course through newly harvested fields of wheat stalks.

We unwound the car windows and waved Grandad a cheery goodbye. But he only waved half-heartedly back, suddenly looking very old and very tired. This time there was no disguising the sadness in his face.

This was a man who had been a naval engineer on the HMS *Prince of Wales* in World War II. A man who stayed on deck to the end as it sank, having been torpedoed by the Japanese in the South China Sea. A man who had been forced by circumstances to physically throw his terrified shipmates into the water to stop them from going down with the ship. And who then had to jump into the bloodied waters himself and watch friends around him be eaten by sharks. A man who was rescued after thirty-six hours in the water. And who then escaped from where he had been taken to recover in Singapore only hours before he would otherwise have been marched across south-east Asia as a prisoner of war, probably to his death. A man decorated with the Royal Navy's rare Distinguished Service Medal for 'zeal, patience and cheerfulness in dangerous waters'.

Yet I had never seen him cry, even when we asked him about the warfare he experienced. He didn't weep when he told me how my grandmother had died. His eyes stayed dry at her funeral, although we all knew how devoted he was to her. This was the first and last inkling I ever got of his capacity for tears.

At that moment I realised for the first time the enormity of what I was about to do: to emigrate to Australia; to abandon my family and friends in the Northern Hemisphere.

What am I doing, leaving England for good?

Meg somehow knew what I was thinking and turned to me, her face full of compassion.

'Don't worry, Jim; you'll see your grandad again. And he'll hate *me* for dragging you away from England, not you', she said. But then she paused for thought. 'Actually, no, that's wrong. It will be *you* he resents for deserting him in his elderly frailty, you unfeeling, heartless bastard.'

I laughed at her feigned venom; Meg always knew how to defuse a painful moment with humour. But the relief of laughter only lasted a brief moment before the doubt and the worry returned. This time there was too much underlying truth to Meg's levity to ignore. The knowledge that I was abandoning my grandfather would gnaw away at me until it was too late.

We turned on to the potholed tarmac road and Meg pushed the accelerator down hard. I stared through the windscreen at one of the large hay rolls lined up in the farmland that surrounds Grandad's property, punctuating the landscape like golden note heads on a music score. As we traversed the level crossing that marked the end of his domain, it felt as if I was not just crossing the railway tracks but my own personal Rubicon. I hoped that I was making the right decision to follow the girl I married back to the country where she belonged. I had not guessed how hard leaving would be. And we had not even started travelling to the other side of the planet yet.

But this was not the time for self-doubt. The decision, however difficult, had been made. It might destroy my friendships, ruin my marriage and tear the relationships within my family apart. Or our lives might be changed incomparably for the better. There was only one way to find out.

***

T MINUS TWO DAYS: DEPARTURE

In transit

The taxi sped down the hill and around the bend towards Lower Richmond Road. An uncharacteristically beautiful sunset infused the whole western half of the sky with pink-grapefruit and blood-orange light. The Roehampton social housing blocks were silhouetted against the dying sun, forming a distinctly less glamorous version of a miniature Manhattan skyline.

'I can't believe it, it's almost like an Australian sunset', said Meg.

I agreed, momentarily worrying that it might foreshadow decades of iridescent English sundowns to follow once I had left the country.

Fat chance. We're talking about the English weather, here. Get real, son.

On closer reflection, it was more likely to be the final swan song of a Northern Hemisphere sun that had belatedly realised its slack attendance over the last twenty-five years. It was trying to make up for its poor prior performance one last time. But its beauty added shallow doubts to my ambivalence as regards the upcoming flight.

'This sunset even makes the Eastwood Estate look good', said Meg.

I laughed and forced the doubts back to wherever they had come from. One decent sunset could not make me change my mind now. I ran past these council estates every evening for the eight months of winter each year that we had lived in Putney. In the horizontal rain, sleet or gusting wind of November they resembled the forlorn Soviet apartment blocks of Yekaterinburg, or any other industrial city in the Ural Mountains. I could not let one pink-and-magenta-hued sky make me see suburban London through rose-tinted spectacles.

So as Meg turned away to resume the daydream that she had briefly interrupted to draw my attention to the heavens, I gazed idly at the impatient traffic accompanying us on our road to departure. We drove on through south-west London and over Kew Bridge, which was its typical mixture of car horns, emergency sirens and normally sanguine people waving clenched fists at each other through the side windows of their Audi or BMW.

'You know, I'm glad we're leaving the country. These roads are as clogged as a Dutch peasant in traditional dress', I said to Meg, with a twinkle in my eye.

'Oh dear', Meg replied, shaking her head slowly in resignation. 'You'd better not come out with jokes like that when we get to Australia.'

My nostalgic reverie was shattered when we arrived at the three-lane lead-up to the international terminals at Heathrow. A lost-looking Fiat Stilo had all but stopped in front of us, obviously unsure as to the terminal towards which it should head. But our taxidriver did not care to slow down; he just leaned on the horn and steered out of the way at the last minute, missing the Stilo's rear light by a matter of inches.

At ninety miles an hour, for Christ's sake. He could have killed us all.

'Fucking wanker', our driver exclaimed. I knew at that moment that I would also miss the politeness, prudence and tolerance that the British are noted for abroad.

A couple of minutes later we emerged, shaking with adrenaline, from the Volkswagen that had whisked us at breakneck speed to the airport and almost to our deaths. Instead of the driver, we thanked our lucky stars that we had survived the journey so far. We paid over our last thirty-five pounds sterling in cash and stepped into Terminal Three.

***

THE ENGLISH INQUISITION

Having passed through Check-In and Security without incident, we walked towards Duty-Free. We must have been looking around shiftily because an official-looking lady approached us near the Customs desk. I instantly thought over the contents of our luggage and tried to work out what we might be unlawfully exporting. The lady explained that I was the twenty-fifth passenger and, as such, I was to be subject to questioning on the details of my journey.

Our emigration-lady's hands were shaking perceptibly against her clipboard and it was clear that she was significantly more nervous about the upcoming bout of interrogation than I was. The first few questions were relatively easy: nationality (British), age (thirty), marital status (just married), sex (as I was saying, I just got married, so what should I say—'plenty'?). As soon as we got to 'purpose of your journey', however, it was a different story. When I said the fateful word, 'emigration', there was a buzz of excitement and frenzied searching for another form ensued.

Now it was questions about the amount of money I was taking away with me (next to nothing) and transferring later (a little bit more), my occupation (lawyer) and so on. I found myself involuntarily summarising the biggest event of my adult life to a complete stranger for the purposes of some bureaucratic fact-finding exercise. I would be a nameless contributor to a great work of statistical boredom. Some obscure migration historian might one day peruse my details as part of their research. Maybe this was the best I could hope for in life, but in my hubris I hoped not.

Suddenly my angst and heartache seemed incongruous, my previous doubts out of place. What was the big deal after all? I was just another statistic; another piece of data to be analysed, interpreted and presented to a desk officer in an impenetrable government report with a title such as 'Detailed personal traits of every twenty-fifth Briton leaving the country in 2004'. Look out for it on the Home Office website, in case you have difficulty sleeping one night.

***

GOODBYE, GREEN AND PLEASANT LAND

Our flight was finally called. Meg went first, on to Singapore Airlines Flight 321 to Sydney. I then followed her, down the gangway—or should I say the gangplank—on to the ship of my transportation.

The fuchsia sun had now set over Hampton Court Palace, Richmond and the Thames. It had also set on the first phase of my life.

I was leaving the home of my ancestors for a distant *terra incognita*. I was leaving the land I loved for the love of my life. Australia, adventure and an unpredictable new era lay ahead. I didn't know how it would turn out, but I couldn't wait to find out.

***

T MINUS ONE DAY: BEFORE SUNRISE AND ARRIVAL

Purgatorio

The thing about drinking on planes that is not generally acknowledged is that it makes long-distance air travel vastly more bearable. Two Asahi beers and you're convinced that *Scary Movie 4* is the funniest film ever made. *Crocodile Dundee III* is a timeless masterpiece. The twenty-two year old Mancunian lass in the seat just over the aisle next to you no longer has an annoyingly stridulous chainsaw of a voice, but a beguiling lilt to her utterances. Your wife looks like the most beautiful woman you have ever set eyes on and you cannot keep your lustful gaze away from her discreetly swelling blouse. And the best part of it is that it is all free (apart from the 670 quid you forked out for the flight), which makes the beer taste just that little bit better.

There is one advantage that strong Japanese lager onboard a Boeing 747-400 does not have, though. It cannot change the fact that the flight from the UK to Australia is an interminably long one. Unless you are focused narcissistically on your once-in-a-lifetime emigration experience (as I was), no matter how many in-flight movies you see, no matter how many aeroplane meals you half-eat and no matter how many glasses of Chilean chenin blanc you gulp down in addition to the Asahi, nothing can prevent the thought that it is more likely that you will die of old age before you reach Sydney than as a result of a failing engine or a terrorist bombing. Well, you hope so anyway, during the bouts of turbulence over the South China Sea. So there is nothing else to do but to try and get some fitful, unsatisfactory sleep, sitting upright in an uncomfortable chair next to a row of complete strangers who, for all you know, are absconding from the law and will rob you during your slumber.

Perhaps I was being unduly wary. There was no reason to suspect, unlike in the rather different circumstances of 1788, that I would be surrounded by felons who had developed a somewhat different perspective on the English legal system than I had acquired professionally as a city solicitor. But I drifted off with the thought in the back of my mind that thieves and fraudsters had travelled this route before and there was no guarantee that the reincarnated soul of one of them did not inhabit the person of a fellow passenger in the seat next to me.

***

FOLLOWING IN THE FOOTSTEPS OF THE FEARFUL

I awoke from a gruesomely violent nightmare, probably from watching too many horror scenes from a low-quality, high body count carry-on movie before closing my eyes. But the more superstitious part of me suspected it might be the residual collective unconscious of generations of convicts, who had made the same insufferable journey as I was now making, infecting my mind with somnolent paranoia.

The bad dreams fortunately dissolved as quickly as the soluble aspirin I'd had the foresight to include in my carry-on luggage. But they were replaced by the equally nightmarish experience of an aeroplane breakfast. The plasticky omelette, superheated baked beans, soggy onions and stale bread were probably not much better than the fare of salt beef and biscuits that had sustained the First Fleeters on their last morning before arriving on Australian soil over two centuries ago.

But the small oval window out of which I gazed afforded a somewhat different view to that of the convict quarters on the HMS *Sirius* in 1788. Back in those days the rolling horizon of unending blue would have mixed with the sight of human effluent coursing below decks. A sharp intake of breath at the impact of the lash on one's back for some minor onboard misdemeanour would have delivered to one's senses, preternaturally alert as a result of the pain, an olfactory melange of the aroma of faeces and a not-so-faint waft of vomit. The putrid stench of closely confined humanity would have mixed with the omnipresent fear of a future whose only certainty lay in the likelihood it would not be pleasant. But for me the first hesitant rays of the antipodean sun burst through heavy nimbostratus cloud cover to illuminate a steely osmium sea. The sweet morning light reflecting off Australian waters distracted me away from reflecting on the less savoury aspects of Australia's maritime past. We were much lower than I had thought and I realised we were only moments off landing.

'I wonder how I'll feel about going through Immigration as a permanent migrant to Australia', I said to Meg. 'It's a pretty seminal moment in my life.'

'It'll be wonderful, Jim. It's your new home', she replied. 'Enjoy the moment while you can. This kind of thing doesn't happen twice.'

But then a look of grave concern crossed her face. I suddenly feared it wouldn't even be a moment that would happen once. Our mood of excited anticipation changed to immediate terror in an instant, as half the wheels of our Boeing 747-400 hit the tarmac and the left wing dipped dangerously. Images of a burnt-out wreck of a jumbo jet spinning out of control across the runway rushed through my mind.

CNN will have a field day. Al Jazeera will watch their ratings soar with delight.

I had just enough time to think how unfair it all was that I had gone to so much trouble to get to Sydney only to die pointlessly on the bitumen before having savoured Australia's delights. But then the pilot somehow got a grip on the aircraft: the wings levelled out, the right-hand wheels met the ground and a huge collective sigh of relief reverberated throughout the plane. A smattering of nervous giggling followed. Meg took my hand in hers.

'Welcome to Australia, sweetheart', she said.

She gave me one of those smiles that had made me agree to leave my homeland in the first place and I grinned back. The twenty-four hour plane journey from London was finally complete and we had made it to Sydney safe and sound. I would stay true to my promise to Grandad and write my first diary entry once I had cleared Customs and Immigration, but for now there was just one overriding thought dominating my mind.

England is over. Australia lies ahead.

The Professor and the Poet

Tina Tin Lap Leung

the professor killed the poet
softly, slowly, gently,
four years of cyanide poisoning
from blue ink and leather-bound books.

professor locked up his muse
and shouted verbose abuse
at the poet who was used
to ra-rhyming freestylin'

'i don't see the need
to reference my ideas', said he.
'nothing is new, so
who cares who said what?'

so the prof made him read
Weber and Foucault then Freud
'i'm learning fuck-all', says poet,
'this Austrian needs a shrink!'

but as the days went by
he knew his muse had died
alas, he couldn't even think
in anything but discourse.

the poet gasped his last breath
as his soul was wrenched
upon the *tabula rasa*, on
subtextual suds he slipped and fell.

French beret flying
he sat there dying
'I am Bic, the pen tamer ... ter'
was his last verse.

Out of Egypt

Cathleen Inkpin

I was born in a cyclone. That's what Dad says.

Dad explains a lot of things with cyclones: why we move around so much, why my hair sticks up on end on bad days, and where Mum went.

All this and I have never even seen a cyclone. I picture it some days: a rolling grey monster feeding on families, crunching their bones like toast, ripping the earth into uselessness.

Dad is driven by the cyclone. He acts like we move in its wake—every new town a new place for Dad to fix up. He calls himself a 'fixer' and no one has yet worked out how to turn that down.

*

The thing about how Dad works is … impossible to explain.

He can turn himself into a well; a fathomless well of stillness. In each new place he'll scope out somewhere—a cafe, a bench, the steps at the bottom of a church hall—and he'll stop there. There's no hunger or desperation in his motions to turn discomforted eyes away. He'll sit with his eyes closed, in all weather, a startling, quiet presence in the middle of town.

It's weird.

*

We arrive in this new Old Northern city during a heavy mist. There's a sticky layer of growing frost on the pavement that trips my feet when we get off the bus.

Dad heard of someone with an open door policy for friends. His name is Ant. He has a round, ruddy face that smiles even when he's confused and his house is small. But he offers a pull-out couch, an armchair and some Dr Pepper. Dad commiserates with him about the match results before he goes to bed. It's after midnight already.

Later, when the blankets are up over my chin, Dad is in the glow of a corner lamp reading a book. He stops and bends the spine over the arm of the chair.

'Pine, you awake?'

'No', I say.

'If you want to go to school tomorrow, Ant says there's one up the road.'

I don't want to think about it.

Dad lives on curiosity. But sometimes I think that's all I am in the world: a curiosity, never around long enough to be anything else. All the questions in all the schools just tend to reinforce that.

The stranger's lounge room is crouching in, the walls bending with cold air. I tuck the blankets under my toes.

'Maybe. Goodnight, Dad.'

*

Being the child of a cyclone is the reason why I sometimes feel like I'm going to fly apart. Days like that my bones feel too big for my skin, a persistent stretch echoing through my body like I need to run and find some empty place where this growing thing inside can break out. Instead, I bite my nails. I bite the skin around my nails. I drum my bitten fingers on any stable surface.

You'll say it's anger or anxiety; this thing that comes out those days. In my world it's neither of those things. It's a space waiting to be filled. It's the waiting, the endless waiting for some unknown fulfilment I might never find.

I blame Dad for that. Our travelling is vague and uncertain, but his purpose is absolute. The days after we arrive in a new place Dad is filled up with excitement and conviction. That's the time when I feel I'm missing something the most.

*

The school is three big blocks of concrete. When the teacher reads the register half the names are met with silence. I can't help thinking that those names made the right decision. It is sunny outside, not that you'd know it through the layers of muck on the windows. They probably painted the school yellow, once upon a time. It's all gone to grey.

My decision today was to keep my head down and ignore the questions. To make sure I can leave this town without shedding a tear.

That was the plan.

It was going well until this obnoxious guy in a puffed-up red bomber jacket sat down next to me at lunch, announced himself as 'Joe' and started telling me all these stories. He didn't ask me a thing, Joe, just told me everything he knew about everyone else. It was backwards that way, so I liked him.

'You like telling stories.'

He wiped his mouth with the back of his hand, nodded so his hair fell in his face.

'We all do, up here. Keeps you warm, like a camp fire you carry around with you. Best part is you never know which stories are true. You just tell all of them long enough, enough times, and they warm you up, pack of lies or not.'

I said, 'I don't like lies'.

Joe looked like he considered this for awhile, not like he agreed, just like he was figuring something out about me. He still didn't ask any questions though.

'So I'll tell you a true story, then', he said. 'You'll like this one; it's tragic.'

He told me about this girl he grew up with who lives a block away from him. They walked to school together until one year ago she stopped going. She stayed in her house and she has never left. The family say she is sick and they have doctors around sometimes, but they don't say what she has or why she can't leave her bedroom. People call and she refuses to talk to them.

'She's our Lady of Shallot', Joe said. 'You know, the curse.'

I could understand that: the lingering grey; the slow movement of days; the strange feeling of entrapment, of dreams stifled; the joking stories that always end with a bruising. I haven't grown to like it up here, yet.

Joe switched focus without blinking. 'You should come to the river on Friday. It's where some of us meet at the end of school, for a laugh. There's this big cave.'

'Yes', I said. 'All right.'

It was Wednesday today and it was like Joe already knew I wasn't coming back if I could help it. That knowing was enough to coax me out. I hate to turn down an adventure.

*

I told Dad about the girl, said how her name was 'Alice'. I said I didn't know where she lived but maybe I could find out, swing by.

'Good job', Dad said. First time he's said that.

These are the things Dad and I look for: the lost ones, the lonely ones. They always seem to find us, even when I'm trying to have a day in hiding. It's one of those things, like looking sideways through a mirror.

*

Joe didn't tell me about the mud.

Here we are: a dozen teenagers playing at being adults, sitting under an overhang where the river stops, sitting in a layer of mud and no one seems to care. There's the light of cigarettes and the warmth of whisky and for awhile everyone thinks they're wise. Only there's Diet Coke to take the bite out of the whisky and it's not long before the effects turn everyone laughable again, back to their real age and then younger.

When I arrived I almost turned back around again, seeing the cluster of knees and eyes, the familiarity of it all.

I'm sitting here watching the way these kids run over personal boundaries: the inside-out quality of their jokes, the ruffles of hair, the catches of eyes. They know each other so well. They live in the same story. It should make that blustering wild thing inside me whip up. Instead I just put my hands in the mud and watch them talk.

Everything is history and family and love in this place. Everything in loops and circles. I know then that it's the weather that makes this place brittle—nothing else. I've been to so many empty places on the road and this city could vanquish them all. I could forget them, sitting here in the dark, in the mist and chill. I could fill myself up with stories and history until I'd never been anywhere else. I could be born here. I could be born from the mud.

That might be the whisky talking, a Northern lie that feels like the truth.

Sometime into the night that is really morning, Joe breaks away from a girl, from her hand held in his, to put his next to mine in the mud.

'What are you thinking, thinker?'

'That girl', I say. 'Just thinking about that girl. What's she missing?'

'An ordinary night with ordinary people.'

The noise in our overhang is a warm blur: there's a couple kissing, three guys with their legs stretched out talking about tomorrow and only tomorrow. And Joe's voice.

Ordinary to Joe is foreign to me. I should tell him that

it's something worth holding onto, but to point that out will change it and I wouldn't want to change this.

'Can you take me to her?'

'Tomorrow', Joe says, like he realises, intuitively, that tonight is not for a greater purpose. He can keep tonight for me. I can't keep it for myself.

*

Dad has cracked his eggshell into his egg again at breakfast. It's a sign.

'Nothing doing?' I ask.

Dad shrugs and his shoulders are heavy. 'Give it a few days, but I'm not sure there's anything to fix here.'

Maybe we're the ones who need fixing, I think. Dad keeps us moving for a reason. This place doesn't need fixing. I like it. It's worming its way over me.

'I'm going to meet that girl, tonight.' It's my only trump, this tiny story about a closeted girl.

Sure enough, a small smile graces the sides of Dad's mouth. He swirls his spoon in his coffee and when Ant comes in the door he takes it out to point in my direction.

'Great girl, my daughter', he says. 'Chip off the old block.'

I roll my eyes out of obligation and Ant laughs in the same way, but the wink in my direction is genuine.

*

'Did you love her?' I ask Joe as we stroll the block from his house.

'No.' Joe throws his head back and laughs from his heart.

'I think you're more in love with her in a few sentences than I ever was while knowing her.'

I don't say anything to that. It's true.

'What do you think she looks like?' he says, slowing our pace so we don't reach the end of our short walk too soon.

I push him off the pavement, playful. 'Face like a moon', I say. 'Pale, tall and awkward.'

Joe laughs again, like I'm his favourite toy. 'Not even close. Freckles, dimples, soft all over.'

'All over? You sure you weren't in love with her?'

'In another life', he says. 'Not this one.' And he points across the street, upwards at a window. The curtains are open and a lamp is casting a soft glow. We wait on a wall together.

'I feel like a criminal', I say after awhile, uncomfortable, excited.

'Don't worry', he says. 'She's used to it. People get curious.'

Some immeasurable time later the girl appears like a papal audience, looking out, her nose almost touching the glass. We're under the lamplight and Joe raises his hand, waves. She waves back. It's not antisocial. It is strange and horrible and lovely. She's smiling and she doesn't look sick. It's hard to believe she never leaves that room. I want more than anything to meet her.

After awhile she draws the curtains and the light goes and a loss that wasn't there before comes over me.

'There', Joe says. 'Now you know all of us. Our strangest and', he points to himself, 'our most lovable'.

'I'm writing her a note', I say.

I do. It says, 'Can I come up?' and I post it through her letterbox with my number scrawled at the bottom.

'She won't answer', Joe says. 'She never does. She likes it

up there. She likes to be away from everything and somehow part of it at the same time.'

'No', I shake my head. 'It's just what she knows; she's forgotten there's anything else.'

Joe looks at me, his lips gone shrewd. 'She's not you.'

When I don't reply, Joe says, 'Come back to my place, we can watch a superhero movie and get you out of that head of yours. What you need right now is lots of explosions'.

'*Spider-Man*', I say. '*Spider-Man* or I'm going home.'

'You make so many demands of me', Joe says, but he's grinning.

This place is all wrong. It seems cold, but everything in it is like firelight.

*

The message comes the next night.

It says, 'no'.

Joe was right.

*

Dad comes home with an appetite for the next week and his hands are worked. He's fixing houses this time, instead of people.

'How's it going with that girl?' he asks one morning, when I crawl out of bed with mud still under my fingernails.

'I'm not sure.'

'That's a good sign', he says and his smile seems easier than usual.

*

Joe catches me typing a message while avoiding the footballs flying by my head. I gave school another chance and it seems like others did as well—there is more noise in the halls. It's the middle of term and the middle is always the most joyful.

'Are you talking with her now?' he asks.

My phone beeps and he swoops it out of my hand.

'"I prefer summer"', he reads. '"I've never been to the beach, but I imagine it".'

I would have liked to read that one the first time just for myself. Still, there's a glimmer of awe in Joe's eyes that I bask in, until I realise he's typing a reply. He holds the phone high above his head to write it, out of my reach.

'I can take you', he types. 'Come down.'

'Joe!'

Joe just smiles that smile that charms the girls' hands into his, a sure smile.

The phone beeps. Joe reads it silently and then tosses the phone in the air. I catch it before it smashes on the concrete.

'You can thank me later', he says.

*

Alice doesn't walk like a sick person—she doesn't wobble—and her skin is fair. Then again the only chronic illness I have experienced is fear; that cyclone fear driving my family outwards.

'You don't look sick', I say.

'I know', she replies. There's no guilt in it, which means it's true. She is ill. I don't like thinking about that.

We take a bus and then a train and then another bus and then we have to walk to get to the ocean. All that time we are travelling, Alice is asking me questions. You'd think I'd hate this interrogation, but there's a difference to the curiosity of someone who has hidden from the world; there's no judgement in the way she gets me to unravel my life in-between bus stops.

Alice takes a long time to walk; the only outwards sign of illness.

'What does it feel like?' I ask.

'Heavy', she says. 'And at the same time, like I'm floating. It's a dreary kind of tiredness; like the weather. That's why I prefer to stay indoors.'

'And not feel it?'

Her eyes are sharp when they come up to match mine. I've caught her there, on that agonising precipice: the decision to feel everything—the heavy, floating, wonderful, painful everything—or to stay in a tiny world she can control.

'Let's go to the beach', she says.

There we are. I look away from her. At the end of the road is a hill and down some steps there is beige sand and a churning ocean.

The wind is large and growing. It spins the ocean white and I curve into Alice without thinking; into the dips and arches of her, the softness all over.

'Will you stay?' one of us asks.

The wind spins and wheels. I close my eyes, hold on tight and think about running back to the bus stop. Rain falls and we are a clinging mass of confusion. We could fly apart in this; it could be our ruin.

Instead the wind moves on and we are still there.

'I'll try', someone says. I think it's Alice, her voice so close she is in my skin.

*

Another day drops, windless, free.

'Pine', Dad says beside me, our feet submerged in mud. 'About that cyclone …'

I have brought him down to the river and it's a misty morning, the sun only a dream behind it.

'It's okay, Dad', I say. 'I know.'

The cyclone was a story. That's all it ever was, but it was our story.

'We can stop now, I think', Dad says. 'We can stay, if you like.'

'My feet are cold', I say.

He grins at me and together we pull our feet from the mud and walk back into the mist, reborn.

I Am a Writer

Conor Bateman

I am a writer,
A writer of fictions,
I am the heart that you call home ... *

It's late. I know this not from the blinking LED lights on the clock at my bedside but rather by my writing style. When it gets late, things just start appearing in my work. It's not bad, no, not by any stretch, but it brings things back to me; memories of a distant past. Sometimes it's pleasant: I can bask in the warmth that was my childhood, my relationships ... *that* relationship. But other times it hits hard, and it's not like I can break away from this train of thought because when you're sitting at your typewriter at 2 am and the only sounds are the cabs down on the city streets and the keys tapping away at your subconscious, you can't stop to organise, to plan, to recreate. It's all the truth.

So right now, at this very moment, I have killed Colin. He is lying on the floor of his newly furnished apartment, a crumpled heap on the IKEA carpet. It's not easy to kill someone you know. Sure, maybe it's harder to actually kill someone, to drive a dagger into someone's spine in reality—that I can admit. But in writing, it's not just the sense of physical death that is drawn out of the ink on the page; it's the emotional death, too. You see, all that this person is—what they want, who they meet, even to the extent of hypothetical sight—can only be known by the author. A reader sees a compelling character's demise, whereas a writer sees a friend moving away forever.

Colin isn't the first of my victims. It's a shame, really, that twelve people have been sacrificed in the name of fiction. And they weren't bad people. Sure, they may have started off a little rough around the edges; that's what first drafts and a lack of intense editing do to the front end of a novel. But as they progressed, as I progressed with them, they became better people. I made them better people. Then I threw them away.

Normally the dogma of karma would lead us to believe that by saving a life you ensure that someone will save yours. That was not the case for Katrina. She had troubles at home: she never got along with her mother, a single mother I might add, and she rebelled. She trudged through her teenage years, searching for something, some strain of familiarity or sense of companionship, to no avail. She excelled in academics, but rejected all notions of her intelligence. She ended up as a doctor, detached from the people, thinking of them only as patients. Yet when Rita—a woman Katrina saw every day on the park bench across the street from her hospital—was in dire need of medical attention, Katrina fought for the woman's rights. She ignored Rita's lack of health insurance, treated her and saved her life. In a sense, Katrina's death was ironic. While saving a life, she contracted a life-threatening disease herself, and the disease won.

I knew Katrina for a year and a half, Colin for only six months. I knew Shane for three weeks (it was a short story) and I knew Kane for over two years. Some of them died in hospital, others at home, some in freak traffic accidents and one on top of an IKEA carpet. So it goes. I guess, in essence, I couldn't keep a hold on these people who I could count as my closest friends. It's our own little journey through their lives that perpetuates mine.

In times of hopeless reminiscence it's only natural to question why I still do this. Why I write. Specifically, why I write in such a manner. I am detached from the real world; my only link is my publisher, and I believe that is for the best. How could I kill Colin and Katrina and Shane and the rest if I could walk down the street and know them? To see them in reality would crush me. In fact, the irony of my own situation is that those I write about, or at least mirror images of them, are the ones that purchase my books. They actively seek my books out to see how they will end—the level of tragedy, the circumstances, the losses. You see, it is society's penchant for sorrow and depression that forms my market. And that in itself is depressing.

So with Colin dead I now have to form a conclusion: whether I leave it here in a moment of heightened poignancy or elaborate in recollection, reinforcing the loss the reader has just felt. To be honest, I just don't know what to do at this point. You see, Colin was a writer. He wrote novels based on everyday people in everyday situations. I guess you could say he was a literary realist. He had a unique taste in film and music. He was single, after a crushing break-up years earlier. He was introverted, shy and intelligent. And now on the floor of his apartment he lies unmoving. And in the normalcy of such an occurrence why do I find it hard to conclude this tale? Because I am Colin. *I am a writer. A writer of fictions. I am the heart that you call home ...*

> *And I've written pages upon pages,*
> *Trying to rid you from my bones,*
> *My bones, my bones.**

* From 'The Engine Driver' by The Decemberists.

N

Edita Pahor

I had a dream
It was about the preposition 'at'
I saw it like someone clinging to a smooth cliff
Freshly out of language
    a new babe
Fighting for its meaning.

In Stormy Visions

Elisabeth Murray

Mrs Iris Clutter heard her daughter coming down the hall. She sat down at the table and poured a glass of water that immediately frosted and dripped on her plate as she drank. Grace came in, reading a book of poems. She sat down without taking her eyes off it and began tapping her fork against her plate as she mouthed the words like some pagan chant. This irritated Iris. She started to eat and realised she had been clenching her teeth. Then Grace looked up, as though she had inexplicably materialised there.

'Did you go down to the post office today?' said Iris.

'No, I got too caught up in "Adonaïs".'

Iris paused. Sometimes she thought her daughter tried to provoke her just for an excuse to brandish that unholy gibberish.

'All right, well, you'd better go tomorrow. I don't want poor Jonathan having to come all the way up here again.'

As they ate, Iris looked at her daughter out of the corner of her eye. She was twenty-seven and went about in jeans and scuffed shoes and t-shirts with childish prints. In fact Iris suspected her daughter had never been with a man. Of course Iris had always told her to wait until she was married, that all men thought of only one thing when they looked at a woman, but now she wondered if she mightn't have felt more at ease if she knew her daughter was carrying on with a dozen men. Well, a half-dozen. Otherwise how long could a person sit locked in their bedroom before they became a psychoneurotic, withered recluse?

After three aborted ventures at university Grace did nothing more than work her way through boxes of books she ordered off the computer. The boxes irked Iris in a way she couldn't account for. She had once picked a book out of one on the kitchen table and it was grim and unnatural and somehow sinful. Tucking it back she felt slightly ill, as though she had glimpsed down a hole an animal's mangled body. Every box was like a shameful house guest who was insidiously corrupting her daughter.

As Iris collected the plates she watched Grace going through the doorway, thick-waisted and sullen. She was not an easy girl to love. At times like this Iris missed her husband so much it was like she had lost him all over again.

She opened the window as she washed up. There was an expanse of grey to the west. It was like this everyday in summer: heat that seemed to come from the very core of the earth, the sky like the lid of a saucepan. Then the heat would condense and everyone would be dripping and the sky would look like rain, dark and pregnant as a rat's belly, but it would never come.

She stared out over the bald lawn. She remembered the last time her husband had mown it and the grass had never grown back, as though it knew she couldn't have borne yanking the machine to life and driving it around with its roaring never matching the roaring in her own head. Roaring of outrage. Maybe someday it would rain properly and the grass would come up and her husband would come back and he would mow it and she would stand here at the window stirring lemonade and they would have that decency, that simplicity, back.

In the silence the familiar, hazy hope came to her. It was like a slight case of nausea, but she liked it because like nausea it held the promise of being purged; there would be something momentous at the end of it and then finally relief. Looking out at the lawn, dim under cloud, remembering him as richly as if he stood before her, she knew he wasn't dead because the dead are remembered through a kind of mist. She could still feel the heat off his skin, his heartbeat going against her cheek.

It had been sixteen years. She remembered the minute precisely: it was pure and bright as a swimming pool. Iris had once told Grace about it, but Grace said it wasn't real, she had invented it. Iris never mentioned it again, but she knew it was real. No one could dream up something like that; so palpable that when she recalled it there was the taste of dirty sea air, the squalling of seagulls.

They were on holiday in Shortcake Bay and her husband said he was going to the kiosk. Grace was standing halfway up to her knees in the ocean holding the hem of her dress.

She'd loved the sea so much, which had bemused Iris since she herself was a little afraid of it. Grace asked him to get her a Paddle Pop, a rainbow one, because she didn't want to leave the water. And he had gone jogging off—no, first he had kissed Iris properly, unapologetically. And she was watching him under the brim of her sunhat and his muscles were coming up hard and here there was such a pitch of discomfort—the salt and the seagulls and the sun in her eyes—that she thought it must have been some sort of foreshadowing.

They had waited. Grace was impatient and pulled off her dress and Iris held it and watched her plane off through the water. How long had she stood there? It had been like looking through warped glass. Warped by worry for her husband and for her daughter far out in the ocean; worry sealed together like some noxious cocktail.

Iris couldn't help thinking it must be some kind of contrition. Over the years she had built up a catalogue of her every possible transgression. But after all, the idea of repentance was curiously reassuring because with it there would be forgiveness then satisfaction, even some kind of reward. And she could only hope (the sensation so akin to nausea) that it would be in the form of her husband's return.

Grace would rather think he had died or even committed suicide. She had a litany of scenarios and corresponding proofs. But when you looked at it rationally, how likely was it that he'd been killed and no leads had surfaced, no body had ever been found? Grace said maybe he'd killed himself; put rocks in his pockets or jumped off the cliff face and was now so far out he'd never be found. It was as though she went out of her way to talk nonsense and upset her own mother. Well, Iris didn't argue with her daughter anymore. Convincing herself of such an irrevocable conclusion was probably the only way Grace could sleep at night.

The only way Iris could get out of bed in the morning was if she took up that hope again. That her husband might write today, or walk up the front path, or even that a hospital or nursing home might call her—at her most desperate she could hope for that. And she thought of clean, bright places with vases of flowers and games of chequers.

Iris took off the rubber gloves and straightened up. There used to be times when she'd have to dry her face, reapply her make-up and even spray some perfume over the sour smell of tears when going out of a room. But she was dry now as bone.

Out in the living room she found Grace sitting under the lamp, reading. Her mouth moved like a fish's. As Grace looked up, Iris saw with a lurch of her stomach that her eyebrows were dark and clotted and her eyes were like shadows. It was a look almost of rage, as though Iris had pitched a terrible insult or threat. Then Grace looked away, closed the book and put it on the table beside her.

'Love', said Iris. 'I want to talk to you.'

She came into the room and switched on the other lamp.

'Well?' said Grace.

Iris sat under the second lamp. Both of them were facing the television. The screen reflected the lamps like planets. Outside it was almost dark. The curtains were drawn.

'I've been thinking, love. You should really ... I mean, you might want—'

There was a sound of thunder. Grace got up and looked through the slit in the curtains.

'It's not going to rain', said Iris. 'Won't you come back here?' She was dazed by the shank of dark she could see through the curtains. It seemed to have come up so suddenly.

Grace sat down. She picked up the book and ran her hand over the cover like she was going to start reading again, but she looked at her mother, one eyebrow raised.

This was a performance of such familiarity. How could Iris explain to Grace the urgency she felt, when she could decide no excuse for it? She wanted to march over and shake Grace and tell her she should just stop reading, put on all the make-up she could find, get a job in town and wait for the boss's son to marry her. It would be a pronouncement: eloquent, almost biblical in the way it would have her daughter nodding and sitting up and swallowing back tears, but in the same instant seized by a vivid optimism better than any of the nonsense in those books that had seduced her.

Iris closed her eyes. Thunder came again, briefly, coiling away like a man's shout somewhere up the highway. Primal, dissolving.

'You know, I really think it might rain', said Grace.

Iris nodded.

'Will you tell me what you wanted to say?' said Grace. She leaned against one arm of the chair and hung her legs over the other. 'For God's sake, is it about the books? I told you I'll pick them up tomorrow.'

'You must own all the books in the world by now', said Iris, so quickly she startled herself.

'No, mother, I don't.'

Iris could no longer see Grace's face in the screen, but by her tone supposed she'd just rolled her eyes.

'Oh, Grace, the cost—' the words were like a piano piece Iris knew by heart, coming as soon as she put her fingers to the keys.

'Cost, cost, what's money?' said Grace. 'And I'm banking on you to be cashing in your chips soon enough.'

Iris saw the laugh framed on her daughter's face and then there came a knock at the door. Iris looked at Grace, but her head was twisted towards the door. Iris rose. She felt Grace slide past her into the hallway and she said, 'Please stay here, love'.

It was a young man. Iris flicked the porch light and orange pearls of water sprang up on his shoulders and his tangle of hair. It was indeed raining. Past the porch light it came down like a theatre curtain.

'Mrs Clutter', he said. 'I mean, you must be Mrs Clutter.'

'Yes', said Iris, holding the door and watching him uncertainly.

He didn't look like he was from here. He was wearing an enormous backpack but she knew it also from the look of his face, which was brown and fine-boned as though it had been sculpted. His eyes glittered out of his face like bits of gem.

'I'm sorry, I'm Jacob. I'm—'

It was raining harder now. He stepped closer to the door to keep his backpack from getting wetter. He looked at Iris, fully, as though trying to see something at the bottom of her eyes. A scar of lightning appeared in the sky.

'I'm his son', he said. 'Your husband's.'

'Oh, Lord, Bill's?' the words seemed to fall out of her mouth, which was slack and chalk-white. Without being aware of it she stepped back.

As he got closer she felt a stab of the old maternal instinct. He was so young. What had she been thinking, leaving a boy out in the rain like that?

He scraped his feet on the mat and came in. His eyes went straight to Grace.

'Jacob, this is my daughter, Grace.'

'I know. Oh, how great to finally meet you.' His face split into a grin. He seemed to have brought all the porch light in with him. His skin shone like planed wood. Grace stood close to the wall, looking at him. Iris went over to her chair and gripped the arm like a raft. Jacob watched as though transfixed.

'You mean ... What do you mean?' said Iris. Her voice was so soft it could have been missed but for the strain in it; a thin thing that seemed to distend in the air even after she had closed her mouth. She fell into the chair and shook her head over and over. Grace stood by the door, watching him from heavy-lidded eyes.

He spoke as though trying to restrain some kind of thrill. 'Well, my mum lived in Shortcake Bay and she said she met him once on the road. She had a bad alternator and he helped her out and later he used to visit and then she got pregnant. Well, I guess Dad was glad about a new baby, so he just— went.'

Grace looked down the hallway as though she'd heard someone call for her, but it was black. She walked past Jacob to her armchair.

Iris leapt up. 'Jacob, come and sit down. I'm so sorry you got wet. Can I take your bag?'

'No, thanks', he said, putting a hand on the strap. 'It's real heavy. I'll just set it down here.' He sat on the three-seater and put the bag at his feet.

Now Iris couldn't stop looking at him. The resemblance struck her like a blow to her stomach; how had she missed it? He had her husband's pink, honest mouth; those bone-white teeth; the same hard, egg-shaped muscle above his elbow; the same scoop below his Adam's apple where his pulse twitched. It was as though Bill was sitting there before her. It was all she could do to keep from going and sitting close to him; to put her hands over him and feel life going steady under his skin.

Grace said, 'Well, why didn't he tell us? All this time, we've been here. Didn't he try and tell us?'

'Well, I guess that's how life goes', said Jacob. 'Days just go by. And out on the bay time goes different. Maybe he meant to.'

Iris remembered that her husband had suggested that trip. But she felt not one flash of betrayal. So this was what it was to be saved.

'I understand, Jacob', said Iris. 'I'm just glad to know he's—he's all right. Would you like a cup of tea or some cake?'

'I'll get it', said Grace. She jumped up.

Iris wanted to ask Jacob about Bill, to forge him before them from the smallest details. She was glad Grace was out of the way; she wanted none of her gloom or scorn.

There came a scream from the kitchen and Iris rose numbly, panic inconceivable in this new peace.

'You left the bloody window open', Grace spat through the storm as she slammed the window shut.

Like the last word of an argument, a stray wind ripped through and knocked the coin jar off the fridge. It hit the linoleum dully and some of the coins went spinning like little vortexes, vanishing into dark, dust-filled clefts under the fridge and cupboards. It looked as though some very wet, careless person had been knocking around the kitchen. There was a tea towel on the floor and water swilled across the sink and leaked down the cupboard below. It was disturbing that they could have been sitting in the next room while the wind and rain invaded, interrupting and rearranging. Grace was watching the jar, which oscillated on the linoleum like some of the wind remained and was toying with it, or perhaps it was a trickster ghost.

'At least it rained', said Iris.

Grace didn't look up. Rain dripped off her nose and her fringe was blown into disorder.

'Do you want me to get the tea?' said Iris.

'No', said Grace, gazing at the bench as though she had been in the middle of preparation and was surprised to see it empty.

Iris went back to the living room. In her head the coins kept going with that metallic sound and she felt ill. It was Bill's idea, saving for a rainy day, and Grace's face would light up when he got her to count out a dollar and took her to town for a treat. Some of the coins at the bottom were likely his.

Sometimes Iris took the jar to her bedroom and poured it out on her pillow methodically so as not to disrupt the layers of age. She held the coins in her hands and thought them still warm from Bill's and felt for a moment the full flesh of his palm, warming hers from somewhere she couldn't fathom: the past, fantasy, a realm beyond existence? Now none of it mattered because she *would* feel his hands (brown, calloused) and the sick feeling became that hope and she was so close ...

Then Grace came in and the tray clattered onto the table. Iris nudged her away and poured the tea.

'It's great I've got a half-sister', said Jacob, turning to Grace with that white grin.

Grace seemed unable to look away. 'Shortcake Bay is the best place I've ever been', she said. 'Shut inside this place it's like—' She turned to Iris. 'We should move there.'

'Don't be silly', said Iris. She had never seen her daughter like this before. Grace was staring at Jacob like there was an ocean glittering between them. Iris said, in a voice that sounded loud and jarring in the room, 'I can't stand the sea. It's not where we belong. We're good country people'.

Grace said nothing. The words rang in Iris's ears like a gunshot. The grin never slipped off Jacob's mouth.

'You'll stay with us, won't you, Jacob?' said Iris. 'We'd love for you to stay however long you want. Do you have things in your backpack?'

'Yes, I do', said Jacob, patting it. 'I know I should've called, or written, but it was just … spontaneous.'

'No, no', said Iris. 'I wouldn't have believed—I wouldn't have known.'

'I thought you wouldn't', said Jacob. 'Will I sleep on the couch?'

'No!' Iris stood up. 'There's a spare room. Just give me a minute to straighten it out.' The blood rushed to her head as though she had been lying down for years. She tried to get a grip on herself.

'Grace, love, come and help me straighten it out. Do you want a hot shower, Jacob?'

'I'd love it', said Jacob. He hoisted his backpack over his shoulder and followed Iris along the hall.

'I'll take your backpack if you like', said Iris, at the door to the bathroom.

'Oh, no problem', said Jacob. 'It's got my stuff in here. Pyjamas, you know.'

Iris shut the door and stood against it. There was the gush of hot water, the thump of dropped clothes, the sliding of the shower door.

Grace was not in the spare bedroom. As Iris changed the bedclothes she thought of going next door to Grace's room, but she couldn't think of what she might say. She went into the kitchen without looking at the mess and got a glass of water which she placed on Jacob's bedside table. She went around straightening a painting, moving an ornament. In the trivial physical movements she was kept from slipping off into the bubbling darkness of shock.

She heard the taps creak and the clunk of pipes. She closed the curtains, taking a long time about it. When she turned, Jacob was standing in the doorway in boxers, his hair thick and somehow blonder from towelling. In the hall light she saw his arms and legs were covered in real, golden hair. She smelled that clean, male smell.

'To see you here', said Iris, moving away from the curtains. 'To *see* you, I can't tell you ... I wouldn't have believed you if you'd called or written.'

'I thought you wouldn't've', he said.

He seemed so at ease there, even in his boxers, so she didn't feel embarrassed talking like this to a young boy who bore such an absurd but miraculous relation to her.

'It's been so long', she said. 'I didn't know what to do. But I always had hope. I always *knew* because if he'd died I'd have *felt* it. And all along, when everyone else told me ... Now it's like no time ever passed. Maybe I had one hour worrying about him— he was late home from work, maybe—but now everything's the same again.'

Jacob nodded, shifted his weight to the other foot. He smiled.

Iris took a sharp breath. She wouldn't cry now; she didn't want to overload him. There would be plenty of time. Hours, days, years.

'Well, you get to bed, now', she said.

He came into the room. She reached out and touched his shoulder. He grinned at her. She smiled a shaky smile charged with imminent tears and whispered, 'Goodnight'.

Her room was at the very end of the hall. Iris shut the door and knelt by the bed in the dark. Past the gaping curtains the window was black, the moonlight only a smear in the corner of the room. Now and then as she prayed the thunder sounded and lightning came almost immediately behind it; a big rod of light that flared the backyard into a pale sketch of grass and trunks.

Tonight her prayer was another make altogether; tonight she was genuinely thankful. She got into bed and he was close against her: brown, smooth, warm.

*

When Grace woke she thought it was because of the storm, which seemed to have distilled into a crashing wall of rain. Such a thick, unbroken bellow that in the first moments of waking she did not feel real. Compared to the rain she was substanceless.

After a sleep-addled second her senses sharpened. There was somebody in her bed.

Though she was facing the wall, she knew it was Jacob immediately because she had seen his skin that evening. Feeling it on her was like meeting somebody she knew only from letters: it was familiar, as though her prediction had come very close, but still there was something more and she knew then that no thought can reach the feel of a person's flesh.

It was dark, with no suspicion of dawn on the wall. She didn't say anything to him. She lay there as though knocked unconscious, but in truth she had never felt more alive. She had thought she filled that single bed (she could not be called petite), but now it was as though there was some open area behind her she hadn't been aware of—or rather that she had felt for years but could never locate. They fit together like two shells.

His hands were like the sun-warmed ocean: rough in places with salt, but ineluctably smooth; polished by undulations. She could smell the sea off him. She knew he'd showered, but she thought something like that was built into a person's bones.

Jacob didn't speak, either. It occurred to Grace he might be sleepwalking and for a moment she was humiliated, but he seemed so firm, assured, that she could only lie there. Some stirring came up in her, which at first felt like the beginning of tears. Then it was not like crying at all and she fell asleep as though part of her had been consumed.

*

Grace woke again in the light. The gathering heat, the stillness of morning and just her body in the bed. So many times she had woken with this hollow feeling. She had tried to oust it but nowadays tolerated it as a tract of grief; a signpost indicating that she had accepted it. But this morning it was like a stark cavity. In pieces the night came back to her and the bedroom was quieter, the mattress colder, her skin stinging like something had been cut away from her. Words skirted her mind as she lay there: *'Tis we who, lost in stormy visions, keep with phantoms an unprofitable strife—Convulse us and consume us day by day—And the icy earth swung blind.* She could not see why Byron should be attached to Shelley in her head. It bothered her. She tried to recall the rest of Shelley's stanza but it would not come.

She got up. The light came through the edge of the curtains, butter-coloured. She put on a dress, folded into the back of a drawer, which her mother had bought years ago. It was creased and didn't fit her, but she left it on. She brushed her hair out. All this she did so quickly and dispassionately it might have been her daily routine.

Down the hallway she stopped outside Jacob's door. She heard no sound inside. He would be up, she thought. Used to getting up early, living by the sea. When the light came clear as wine, the waves were high and the town lay flat and quiet past the dunes.

Her mother was standing in the middle of the kitchen glancing about as though she had stumbled into someone else's house and couldn't understand how. It was hot. The frypan was spitting. Grace felt like a child attuned to trouble she couldn't unravel.

'Love, come here', said Iris. She took Grace's arm and led her to the living room.

The television was gone. The light now shone on the wall behind, neat and pitiless.

'Where is Jacob?' said Grace, facing her mother. 'You tell me right now!'

Iris stepped back.

'He's not here. I don't know where he's gone, but he's not in his room. I don't know what's happened.'

Grace turned back to the bare wall like a punishment. 'You

do know. I know. We should've known. He was a goddamned liar, bloody imposter, fucking thief!'

Iris stood there. Her face contracted with pain.

'Grace, don't speak like that.' She was not watching her daughter; she was watching some nutty character in a soap opera.

Grace wanted to shake her mother, hear her brain clank in her head. Instead she strode down the corridor and kicked open Jacob's door and stood staring at the unwrinkled bed. She stared at the glass of water, the light twitching through it. She kept staring with some sick compulsion, as though she had prised open a coffin and was glaring in at death.

She shut the door and went back down the hall. Her mother was still standing at the door to the kitchen.

'Where's my book?' said Grace. She started throwing everything off the table by her armchair. She tore out the cushion and got down on her knees. 'He took that, too', she said.

Iris stood there nervously, as though watching somebody else's child throw a tantrum.

'That lunatic took that, too', said Grace, again. She went into the kitchen. 'What else?' she said. 'What else, what else?'

Iris wasn't sure if she was talking to her, or herself, or the shadow of the boy that still suffused the house, or to God who must have seen it all happen.

'Oh, the coin jar!' said Grace and laughed in a way that chilled and saddened Iris at the same time. 'Of *course* the coin jar!' But there was a paler note in her raging sarcasm now.

Iris came into the kitchen and looked at the void above the fridge. 'Didn't they spill last night, love?'

'I picked them up. Every single one. They were here.' Grace's hand went up in a gripping attitude as though the jar might still have been there, but invisible. The television was now some sort of absurd front for what had really been stolen: her book, the coins. Jacob had tried to pass himself off as a real burglar by taking something bulky, halfway-expensive. To excuse what he really wanted.

'I don't understand it', said Iris. 'You mean Jacob wasn't his son? He wasn't Bill's?'

Grace tried to scoff, but her throat hurt. She shook her head.

'But he knew us', said Iris. 'He knew Bill. He was from the bay. He knew us.'

The frypan was squalling, giving off great masses of oil and fat. Grace turned off the stove. The bacon and sausages and tomatoes were withered and dark as dead things. She took a spatula and ate one. As she swallowed she found it was a sausage.

'I don't know, I don't know', she said. Her voice was raw and small. 'Are we good targets?'

Iris leaned against the fridge and a magnet fell to the floor.

'Mum', said Grace and Iris looked up, white. '*We* decay—' the words were naked and broken and all Grace knew at that moment.

Iris nodded. They looked at each other.

'Mum, Dad is dead. Please—'

Iris went over to the screen door as though she had heard somebody knocking there. She went out to the yard. Where there was no grass the lawn was churned by the night's rain. She stumbled, mud almost immediately caking on her bare feet in the glassy sunlight. In the artemisia she vomited and after she'd finished she stood there, bent, with the sky wide over her and the sun cutting down on her neck.

Something touched the back of her neck; she imagined a wavering guillotine. But when she stood up there was a woman outlined by light coming behind her, a spatula dangling from her hand. Blinking, Iris saw that it was Grace.

A Lovely Riverside Place

Mick Beltran

In this district where grasses predominate the land, where
The horizon teases the eye with the curve of our world
A place by a watercourse beckons; come bide time
Of solace and rest; of simply being and belonging

Proudly bearing the scars of its half millennium
Testament to the bounty and ravages of nature, red gum
Its huge girth once marking the banks of this stream, now
midstream but (as in protest) modestly impeding the flow

Tiered branches laden of leaf; limp and languid—but now
Fluid and flashing green, then silver, in the vagarious summer
breezes; reflecting only traces of sunlight upon the myriad
waving faces as dappled sunlight glimmers then fades on
wind-whipped water

The omnipresent calm of this place is broken
Not only by the rustle of the breeze o'er the leaves
But also by a host of cicadas (hidden and unbidden)
Proclaiming delight in the clean dry heat of the day

Rich the river in the sediments of its journey
Green its banks; evidence of recent former might
Contrasting colour, bright to the brown of the river
Half spent in its iniquitous search for the sea

Old broken fences half guarding yards and drab slab dunnies
And amongst the tussocks the remains of the once proud pitch
Obviously so a place favoured by generations past; dreamily
Hear the laugh, and hear the call; and haunting, still, the echoes
of the tribal camp

As the sun pours its soul through the timber and into distance
Shadows lingering and brooding capture these sacred grounds,
Yet eventually are challenged by the ethereal light of night
An ageless act, made merry by the sensuous march of the moon

A lovely riverside place

Bella May

Harriet Westcott

It is five minutes to twelve. I am sitting at my dining room table in the semi-darkness, staring at the clock on the wall. It is one of those old-fashioned types of wooden clocks, with roman numerals instead of numbers. It makes a sturdy tick-tock noise, and chimes discreetly on the hour. It doesn't just look old, it really is. The clock belonged to my mother and her mother before her.

I often cannot sleep. I have found that rather than lying in bed, disappointing myself by not sleeping, it is better to admit wakefulness in a wakeful place. So I sit at my table.

Some nights, I write letters. Long-lost cousins, old school friends and the like are all recipients of my nocturnal kind regards expressed in flowery note cards. I also use the nights to repair clothes. To darn socks, mend buttons and replace faulty zips—my own and other people's—for a small fee. Other times, like tonight, I just sit at the empty table. It is round, like the clock.

I sit in silence and barely make a sound, other than the slight twisting of my hands in my lap under the table. But in my head the regretful thoughts are loud. Over time they come and go, sometimes more demanding than others. But tonight they are speaking forcefully to get my attention. In raised voices.

They ask me why I did it. Why. It is the 'why' question which I cannot answer, and which keeps repeating in my mind. Round and round it goes, like a Hill's hoist on a windy day: sometimes faster, sometimes slower, sometimes in reverse. Like the wind which is always there even on a calm day, the 'why' never goes away—even if I try and answer it, or trap it, or turn it into something else. And like the wind, I cannot control or predict it.

The fact is no matter how often I answer the 'why' question the response is never good enough. I can justify myself as eloquently as I like, but ultimately the real reason is just too hard to bear. Lately I have been unable to avoid it rearing up on the surface of my duly shining dining table in the early hours. For some reason lately the truth has just come right out.

I can chase it away in daylight. Easier to persuade when it is sunny outside. Avoidance is a walk in the park, a trip to the shops for some other necessary errand. But there comes a turning point in the evening when busyness gives way to being. And after that time, which creeps up with the rising darkness, I have no choice but to face it.

It has taken me a long while to realise, to admit to myself, that I was scared about bringing up a baby on my own. How could I do that on my own? My own mother was dead by then and I didn't yet want to be one. It was too early. I had my life to live, before me.

Already I am getting muddled, as I try and get it all out. The reasons all blur into one another, even though I know they should seem separate or follow some linear reasoning of logic. They always flow in a different order, suggesting new connections and causations in multiple variations like a kaleidoscope.

I was young, that much is true. I did imagine that later, at some other time, things would improve. That circumstances would be more conducive to having a child; that there would be prospects or more resources to give the child a better chance. Well, that *we* would have had more resources to do so—because, of course, when I thought that back then, there was always a man around in my future picture.

Of course I know now that this was folly. There has since been no other man.

As I duck and dive back to my past and my past's imagined future, I am almost quite content. I can weave these stories along for hours while the clock on the wall opposite my dining table ticks and chimes away the hours. It is just delusion, though. Another form of avoidance. Because sooner or later 'why' comes back.

It was cowardice, really. Not wanting to face the world as a mum with a baby without a dad. The shame of it: not being married. And that horrible word which they don't use anymore, 'illegitimate'. Of course, things are different now. People—well, women, really—do it all the time; have babies on their own. People don't talk and stare like they used to.

I mentioned that I thought things would get better. The thing was (and I could not have known this at the time) that after that first time, it just never happened again.

The thing was that I couldn't love again, after I had lost.

For a good three, four, maybe even five years afterwards, I was genuinely busy with work and going to dances on Saturday nights. They were fun times, in a way. Though, that was all they were. Nothing more ever happened after the lights came up at the end of the final song and the last few stragglers drifted off home.

At some point I stopped going to these dances, niggled by a sense of inner disquiet and tiredness at the end of a busy week. I began to become aware that the clock *was* ticking. Awareness of this fact was just a fact, to begin with, though not a threat. I simply started looking about me and paying a bit more attention. I put on a bit of lipstick when I went out. I was hoping to catch someone's eye, you see. Not just at dances, anymore.

And I did this for a while: a year, or maybe two.

One morning I found that when I turned my lipstick up it was empty. This bothered me more than it should, and that lunchtime I rushed out of the office to buy another one, in a brighter shade than before. It might have been garish, and it was certainly desperate. I was starting to feel that I was being passed over. I wanted to get noticed. Unfortunately, the combination of these feelings must have somehow manifested and acted as a repellent. A bit like body odour or bad breath.

Then I started to notice the changes, just little things that happened because of the clock, and this made me feel depressed. And at the same time I also felt bitter. It was about this time that I became aware consciously of the 'why' starting. Feeling tired, I went to bed early, but somehow always ended up awake by three just lying in bed wondering. Why. I would drift off by six only to be yanked awake half an hour later for work.

After I retired I slept even less. Rising early—and never one to sloth about—I found myself getting into my car at dawn and driving miles to obscure, distant shopping centres. I would park and wander in without a list or an errand. My eyes would dart about, taking in all the people. And I would wonder about them: where did they all come from? Who *made* them?

One day I caught myself out, staring at a woman drinking hot chocolate in a café, fancying that her hair was like my own. The way she folded and unfolded her legs reminded me of mine under that dining table, one time before, when I was beautiful. Rapt in my fantasy, I had stopped unwittingly bang at the bottom of the escalator and was creating a pile-up of people hastening to get off. The words 'move it, granny' jarred me into reality, and I glimpsed my own ragged reflection in the shop window opposite me. I did indeed look like a grandmother, even though I was not.

I remember that night. I allowed tears to drip over my dining table.

I didn't keep my baby. I should have. I know that now. I should have kept my baby, and loved my baby, and not worried about whether anyone else was talking about me. I should have kept my baby because I could have looked after my baby on my own.

I didn't keep my baby because I was scared of what would happen if I did. I persuaded myself and let other people persuade me that what I was doing was for the best. And even though I would have known then—if I had stopped to listen to my heart—what the answer was without needing to ask why, I didn't let myself have the confidence to do so.

And I have been paying for that for the rest of my life in a currency of sleepless nights.

I've given her a name and I'm not sure if it makes it worse, or better, but in my head I call her 'Bella May'.

Environmentalism

Jimmy Andrews

I
The forest is a single organism.
Although comprising trunks both short and tall,
you can't refract such difference through its prism.
A tree's a tree. Distinction blurs them all.

II
snap a twig
and the whole tree shudders

Liz Goes to Beauty School

Nadia Menon

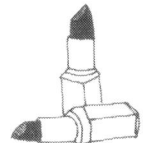

I never really knew Liz Beattie personally. The place where I grew up was large enough to support two high schools and Liz went to the one across the highway. Sure, I had seen her around, and some of my friends might have known some of her friends. It wasn't that big a town and there were only a few places for us kids to hang about. And even though we did go to the same college, it wasn't as if we were ever in the same classes. I was completing an office administration course, with vague ideas of using efficiency and organisation as the springboard into my adult life. Liz, on the other hand, had enrolled in beauty school.

    Liz was a big girl. She was tall and heavy shouldered; her hands and feet were as big as a man's and when she walked her arms would move with a man's promise of strength. Her face was square and broad across the jaw, with straight dark brows. She had dark freckles across her nose, which was incongruously delicate, small and with a whimsical point. I don't remember her ever speaking to me and I don't think she ever did speak too often. But when we were all sitting at the college cafeteria, or on weekends around the mall, you could hear her sometimes: slow and resonant, talking to the couple of girls she kicked around with. She was something of an athletic star in high school; in the inter-school games I played against her in both girls' soccer and hockey and had gotten more than one bruised shin from her cleverly aimed stick. In shot-put and javelin she competed on a regional level. I would hear the boys laugh about her sometimes, but never to her face, and most of the time everyone left her and her crew well alone. The truth was we were probably all a little scared of her.

In the first week of my course I had just organised timetables and rooms and classes and had realised—to my disappointment—that for all of its talk of adulthood, college was going to be much like school. Teachers took the roll and glared if you were late, and you sat at your computer or in rows facing the front, learning things that, mostly, you already knew how to do. I was never a brilliant student but I wasn't terrible either and I had been putting together Excel spreadsheets and PowerPoint presentations in every computing class since Year Seven. At lunchtime I went to the cafeteria and sat with the same girls I had eaten with for the past twelve years. Most of my friends were enrolled in the office admin course with me, some had opted for hospitality and a few of the best-looking or most confident were enrolled in beauty therapy. I was picking at my sandwich crusts and desultorily listening to the general conversation when I first learnt about Liz's choice of future career.

'Oh, hey guys, this is pretty funny. Elizabeth Beattie is in my beauty class.' Janet, who since kindergarten has been the most groomed person I know, leaned back with satisfaction as she held out this news as an offering for the group's amusement.

'Elizabeth who? Oh, you mean that huge girl from Tasman High. Seriously?'

'But she can't do beauty, can she? Don't they have, like, some sort of entry requirement?'

'Yeah. Like looking in a mirror?'

'Yeah and it not fucking breaking.'

'Are you sure?' I turned to Janet. 'I wonder why she'd want to do that.'

Janet shrugged.

'Well she could sure as fuck use some beauty skills', someone cut across. 'Though plastic surgery'd probably be more effective.'

'Her poor customers, though. Like, what would they be thinking? This massive butch bitch coming towards them with hot wax.'

'Oh my god, just imagine her doing your bikini line. Or a Brazilian!'

'Ha-ha, that's probably why she wants to—touching pussy all day. That fucking dyke'd be in heaven.'

I haven't lived there for years now, but I sometimes still get nostalgic for the community that I grew up in. Nearly every kid I went to school with had been born here and though after high school a few of the smart ones had gone to university, most of the rest of us didn't really expect to move too far away. We locals knew this was our place and when I come back I'm always struck by that sense of entitlement.

I can see it in everyone: from the kids sprawled lazily on footpaths in front of shops, to suburban gardeners pruning trees that have had years to put down deep roots, to the old couples going for an evening stroll on the same streets they have walked down innumerable times and who still remember my name and say hello.

Yet even as a teenager I sensed there was a flipside to the security of the place. Traditionally a manufacturing town, the fact that it was set on some pleasant—if not particularly striking—coastline meant that by the time I finished high school there was a steady stream of tourists. The downtown area had been done up by the council a couple of years before and the new mall, according to the local paper, was doing a brisk trade. Still, there was no denying that we were, in all sorts of ways, leagues behind the bigger cities. My mates and I would pore over the clothes in *Vogue* or *Elle* or *Marie Claire* and then settle for whatever we could find in Just Jeans. Sure, the takeaway Euro Sushi was almost as popular as McDonalds, but the Chinese restaurants still served sickly orange sweet and sour pork. Apart from a few old-man pubs there were only a couple of nightclubs where the same kids would hang out and make out and drink too much Jim Beam and Coke and every now and then beat each other up. This was a place where the guys played Rugby League and the girls married young and anyone or anything different was, if not derided, at least determinedly ignored.

The thing then was that Liz had set herself up for a tough time, choosing to do beauty. These courses everywhere are probably much the same, but certainly at my college they were the preserve of the pretty and popular girls. I was always intimidated by them. They had this crispness, everything about them—their hair and clothes and make-up were all so sharply defined. They stood out amongst the rest of us, as glossy as if they had been clipped from the very magazines whose looks they were learning to emulate. It's not that they weren't nice girls. Sure, there were a couple of cliques with a reputation for bitchiness, but on the whole they were attractive and friendly and well-liked. But Liz was always going to be incongruous in that context. I would see her around the place in her black beautician's uniform. Her body, which had had its own strong magnetism, was reduced by the fripperies of scooped necks and nipped waists and tailored skirts into something awkward and misshapen, while the power inherent in her stride was hobbled by a large pair of leather pumps.

One of the very few perks of attending a vocational college is that as a student you get to sample what everyone is studying for very little money. There is a restaurant where would-be waiters fumble your drinks and forget your order; you can buy the lopsided efforts of amateur bakers or get a similarly lopsided cut and colour at the hairdressing school. The beauty salon, offering cheap manicures and skincare and waxing, was always booked days in advance. And judging by the stories that floated around campus, Elizabeth Beattie was no better a beautician than she looked. The main problem apparently was her clumsiness and the fact that she was, simply, so *big*. Customers complained that when she gave them a facial massage she went halfway to crushing their skulls. She once tipped a tub of hot wax over a teacher and the electrolysis machine was out of action for weeks after she tripped over its cord and brought the whole apparatus crashing.

I did have the opportunity of witnessing her in action one time. Janet had persuaded me to come in and pay to let her practise her blackhead removal technique. It was around midday when I went in and the salon, its atmosphere a cross between a hospital emergency room and backstage at the theatre, was bustling.

'Just take a seat for a tick, could you, lovie?' A harried-looking teacher with voluminous streaked hair plopped me on one of those beds which always remind me of uncomfortable medical examinations and promptly forgot about me.

'Elizabeth! When you're ready, please. Your twelve o'clock is waiting; a manicure with the gel colours. And *be careful.*' I noticed Liz, hurrying over towards a customer, bump into the desk as she tried to seat herself and send a display of nail polishes rocking.

'Right, Elizabeth. Remember, the *thicker* file. Like this.' Liz peered anxiously over the teacher's head as she tried to see what was going on. 'You have a try. And quickly as you can, please. You've been behind all day.'

I watched with interest as Elizabeth sat down. Those hands, which had been so lethally assured wielding a hockey stick or curled around the curve of a shot-put, dwarfed the little polish bottle. They were easily twice as big as those of her customer's. To be able to steady her elbows on the desk she had to hunch her whole body in towards its centre. With her brow furrowed in concentration she looked like a worried, monolithic troll.

Sometime later, as I was intent on not wincing while Janet picked at my face with various metal implements, a high screech brought a halt to the salon's activity. 'No! Oh my God, you've just smudged my whole left hand. Why did you put your hand there? I gotta be out of here like twenty minutes ago and I got this dinner to go to tonight … Why the fuck did you put your huge fuckin' hand there?'

'Is there a problem? Oh, Elizabeth, not again! Haven't I told you to leave them until they dry? It's not rocket science. No, no, *no*! Move and let me fix it. Don't just stand there! Can't you do *something* to make yourself useful?'

It was a month or two later that Elizabeth finally cracked. I hadn't actually seen much of her since then; maybe she had decided to keep a low profile or maybe by that time I was already so bored that I was disassociating from the entire college experience. At any rate, it was just before school was due to break for spring and everyone was busy trying to fill their social calendars. Apparently what happened was that a girl had tried to get a brow wax. And Liz, somehow, managed to remove almost her entire eyebrow on the right-hand side. I didn't see the hysterical scene that reportedly unfolded that day at the beauty salon, but I was in the cafeteria the next day at lunchtime when three boys approached Liz as she was waiting in line to pay for her food.

'Hey, you … You, ya tall bitch!' I recognised a boy from either the carpentry or construction courses; a fixture in the group of guys that would hang out the side of the school smoking and occasionally hassling passing girls. 'You remember Heather, don't ya? Yeah, well, she's me girlfriend. And she's, like, a little upset. Cos you ruined her fuckin' face, you fuckin' freak.'

The chatter died down as kids and cafeteria workers alike turned to see what was going on. Liz, however, remained where she was, staring straight ahead. She was looking a little flushed and gripping her tray a little tighter but otherwise gave no sign that she had heard.

'Hey, me mate just asked you something.'

'Yeah, fuckin' answer, ya rude cow. He wants to know why you fucked up Heather's face.'

'Yeah, it's nearly as fuckin' ugly as yours, now.'

'Yeah, that's probably why she fuckin' did it. Cos it kills her that Heather is, like, hot.'

The first speaker had remained silent throughout this exchange. Now, however, with a speculative look on his face, he took a step closer.

'Ya guys know what?' he said slowly. 'You know what I reckon the problem is? It's that this ain't no fuckin' girl at all. What I reckon we got here, guys, is a fuckin' tranny freak.' He was by this time standing right against Liz with his face jutting aggressively up towards hers. I could see fine flecks of saliva land on her face as he spoke. 'I think me boys are gonna have to check this out for me. C'mon, you guys get the arms and let's fuckin' see what this freak is fuckin' hiding between them fuckin' legs.'

The two boys moved in as they were told, but Liz was quicker. Realising that her hands were hampered by the food she was holding, she jabbed the leader smartly under the bridge of the nose with the edge of the tray, lunch and all. As that crunch was echoing around the building she used her now free hands to grab her two other would-be attackers, each in an individual headlock, and whacked them forehead to forehead. For good measure she finished with a powerful roundhouse kick to Heather's boyfriend's already-mangled nose. Having thus disposed of the problem, she stepped over the tangle of blood and boys and chips and gravy at her feet and stalked through the stunned crowd of silent onlookers as haughtily as any warrior queen.

Liz never showed up at college again and I too dropped out soon after. At any rate, at the same time that I was getting a job as an office assistant in the local community centre, learning about graphic design and realising that it was something that I was interested in and could perhaps do well, Elizabeth Beattie was being wooed. Apparently amongst the spectators who stood in the cafeteria was a young man with a passion for martial arts.

I don't live in that town anymore, but I do go back to visit. And whenever I'm there I can't help but notice the Liz and Wayne Kung-Fu Academy that stands on the main drag, only a few blocks away from our old college. It must be doing well because there are spaces for a couple of gleaming new Land Cruisers to park outside. I suppose they need large cars for the kids; Liz has three of them now and they all take after her—tall and stocky and strong looking. I still don't speak to her, and she still doesn't speak all that often, but she seems as content with the lot she has found for herself as I am with mine. It's just that I sometimes wonder: does she ever regret that lost impulse which once led her to enrol in beauty school?

The Boy King

Michelle Retford

Keep your eyes on
the boy with the blue
eyes and large hands,
the one with the trail
of ink stains and
feathers, the one who
appears in the dreams
of strangers, people
he has never met
bend towards him as
he passes.
The innocent boy, the
one with the will to
get what he wants,
the one with the will

to survive all that
comes with it. The
one that will change you,
complete you, undo you,
solve you, restrain you,
guard you, love you
and scare you. Keep your
eyes on the boy,
he'll become like a
second heart, and

that boy, he will
conquer the world.

Supersized Me

Rebecca F Thompson

The night had finally arrived. After a solid week of debating the difficult decision between a cropped miniskirt and tailored trousers, I finally came to a life-changing verdict: a dress. This was a great achievement for me, as my decision-making rationale is somewhat bizarre; I usually select an entirely different option altogether. This strategy was helpful in choosing a spouse, as I was happily able to practise on three separate occasions (I can boast that I have three ex-husbands).

    I gazed at the remarkable woman grinning back at me. I had done a great job: a couple of coats of rigid mascara, some new Beach Babe bronzer, a pale layer of gloss on my lips and I was set. I was ready for my first date in a long, long time. The beauty was a woman who was not me, but created by me and especially for me. My personal reward for the hard work of the evening; I hadn't looked so great in years. Hair: perfectly combed. Eyes: seductive. Lips: simply luscious. Teeth: perhaps a little crooked, but braces were not available during my teenage years. They're really not that bad, although I think the colour is best left undiscussed (let's just say I have had an intimate affair with espresso coffee for the best part of twenty-five years). As my teeth were not able to uphold my otherwise brilliant standards, I allowed myself to move swiftly on. My neck: no wrinkles; all praise goes to my trusty Olay Regenerist cream. Then my gaze quickly passed over my breasts and fell to the pre-loved child-bearing hotel: my stomach. Disaster! I knew what I had to do. I felt a tingling sensation from head to toe.

Kicking off my ugg boots, I crossed over to the other side of the bedroom. My feet tenderly massaged the soft fibres of the carpet. When I reached the majestic chest which dominated the far corner of the room, I carefully coaxed open the highest compartment. I kept my top-secret things in this drawer. It was a little too high for me to reach—after all, I am only 5'2"—but this meant it was high enough to keep the prying children out. I extended my arm to reach inside and lovingly extracted the crumpled package. I took one deep breath and shakily exhaled.

One. Two. Three. Go! Grabbing two oversized corners, I hauled the supersized knickerbockers over my generously portioned stomach. Taking another reassuring breath inwards, I held my pose in front of the mirror. I looked great. It was a complete transformation. I now knew why everyone wore them—I think one could indulge in any number of chocolates and still appear to have lost weight. Note to self: nominate maker of sumo-undies for Nobel prize.

I strutted away from the mirror and picked up the envelope lying on my pillow. I didn't have to be Sherlock Holmes to recognise Eloise's writing. Eloise is, chronologically speaking, my younger sister. However, her maturity far surpasses mine. She is fantastic at dating and providing dating advice and I needed all I could gather for tonight. I was grateful that she used my spare key wisely; to drop off her washing and to leave me little bits of advice. I ripped apart the envelope and extracted the precious letter.

Dani,

I know we haven't chatted in ages, but I guessed you were still looking for your dream man. I thought I'd give you my best tips on surviving the dating world at forty years of age. And then maybe you can preclude this ever-increasing number of exes!

One: I know you have been thinking about it, but don't get a bellybutton ring just to appear younger than you are. A woman does not need any holes in her other than those which are, 'strictly speaking', necessary.

Two: If you're feeling fat just make sure you are seen standing next to a heavily-pregnant woman. Take one with you everywhere you go.

But seriously, Dani, my main parable for you is: if your bloke prefers beauty to brains it's because he sees better than he thinks. Beauty on the inside is more important than on the outside. The beauty you possess is of a sort too frustratingly magnificent not to spill out of you, if you give it half a chance. You deserve the best. Thanks again for doing the washing!

Oh, and don't forget to wear those knickerbockers I bought you. They control your excesses.

Love always,
Eloise.

Well, after Eloise's session of enlightenment, I felt ready to face this date. How could I have separated myself from the fabulous world of dating for so long?

The shrill call of the phone interrupted my thoughts and demanded an immediate answer, but I had to apply the final touches to my physique. I therefore granted permission for the answering machine to do the socialising. In the next room I heard Peter's dulcet tone and I felt my heartbeat elevate slightly—calling only minutes before a date is never a good sign. I crossed the now-pulsating room to listen.

Daniella, Peter here. Can't believe this is happening for the fifth time in a row ... Something has come up. Can't talk now. Maybe talk soon. We will reschedule or something; sometime, somewhere.

I felt myself deflate with the prick of Peter's words. The machine whirred out, melting into the disappointed silence of the room. A somewhat foreign but perfectly manicured hand brushed my now pointlessly glossy lips as I took a measured breath. I reached out for the doorframe behind me, sanctioning its solidity for reassurance. Then a sudden illumination perforated my cloud of delusion: I realised that even I was worth more than this. I was replete after five cancelled dinner dates and therefore Peter was *fini*.

I bolted towards the bathroom, tripping over my discarded ugg boots in a frenzy to reach the basin. I scrubbed and splashed, permitting the cool droplets to minister to flushing face and remove my falsities. I had inadvertently displaced enough water onto the marble surface for it to be dripping down onto my pedicured feet, whereupon I began to recognise my counterpart in the mirror. Emerging from under the beige film was a woman of considerable beauty. Obviously she wasn't a magazine model equipped with a full set of bright, white teeth and perfectly plucked brows to match, but rather a woman who possessed a beauty which surpassed those trivialities.

As I appreciated myself as a woman of honest beauty, I was glad I'd never gone under the knife. My previous desire for a face lift could have left me with some horrendously nasty side effects. Cosmetic surgery can lead to women developing thick Californian accents.

I took a self-assured step forwards and admired my stunning physique. On approval, I deemed it a suitable moment to set free the remainder of my imprisoned self. So, I unleashed the knickerbockers! It was then, as I stood there in all vulnerability, I realised perhaps my physique was not exactly ravishing, but it was beautiful. Yes, there was an inch or two (or three) of extra Me around my middle, but I wasn't a complete catastrophe. I liked what I saw. However, for the time being, I think it still best to include the supersized knickerbockers in my daily attire. And if confronted with an intimate situation where the code of conduct states that knickerbockers must be removed, I need to remember that the dimmer switch is the greatest sex aid ever known to womankind!

I bent to re-read Eloise's letter: it was almost as if she had prophesied the disastrous result of my short-lived relationship with Peter. Despite the feelings of anger and disappointment which continued to corrode the innermost core of my stomach, I felt a sense of freedom. One window had been shut on an undeserving male, but in response a door had been opened. I now had a chance of a better man and, if not, certainly a lifelong relationship with my faithful ugg boots (they have lasted longer than any of my I do's). This wasn't the end, but rather a new beginning—a further progression along the rickety tracks of my heart's pursuit. I was happy; after all, I don't need anything else. I have my three ex-husbands, my two beautiful children, my love guru sister, my devoted ugg boots and my trusty pair of supersized knickerbockers. What more could a woman want?

Ode to CityRail Suburban Carriages (K Set), Emu Plains to Chatswood on the Western Link

Kat de Jong

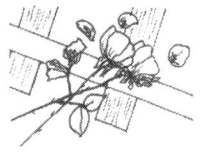

The Train
Is a lousy lover.
Three good thrusts
And it pulls out of the station.

The Future of Books: From Gutenberg to Gadgets

Michelle Willoughby

'Prediction is very difficult, especially about the future.'
— Niels Bohr

Like all good soothsayers (though I do not profess to be good), I must look to the past to see the future. And like all good feminists I believe, still, that the personal is political. I start then with both the personal and the past.

That I—booklover, paramour of the written word, one who lusts for the climactic sigh of the novel's final pages—could come from a bookless heritage is unfathomable, yet true. I look at the 'mark' on her marriage certificate, the x of illiteracy, and wonder how my great-great-grandmother Mary Ann Willoughby, the last Aboriginal-Australian of the Braidwood area, could not know the passions that have possessed me. She was brave enough to secure a 100-acre land grant from the government's Aboriginal Protection Board; she worked the land and mined for gold, but when she died that land went back to the state. She lived for a full nine decades and has many descendants living in the Sydney area, including myself. But never, as far as I know, could she read or write a word.

Perhaps illiteracy is not such a bad thing. After all, books can be dangerous. Drama, melodrama, murder, mayhem and madness are all contained within a book's pages. And from these pages readers have sometimes courted death: think heretical *Bible* lovers who only wanted to read 'the book' in their mother tongue; think Salman Rushdie; think censorship as a kind of death, the demise depicted in *Fahrenheit 451*; the death of fact and the rise of the 'factoid'. Fabulous histories, vainglorious ramblings, sweet science, mindful biographies, prolific research, the imaginary world of the novel—it does not matter what kind of book: to someone, some reader, or sometimes only to the writer, it is worthwhile. In the mind's eye books become real. Synapses fire a world within worlds. Books don't live on pages, they live in our minds. Like a new universe, they expand within the gaps of memory and emotion. Well, the good ones do. In their best form books are revelatory, transformative; in their worst, wasteful. But their future is assured. Assured but not unchanged, books shall live on.

My great-great-grandmother's first child, a son, was born in 1854, the same year in which William Charles Wentworth bequeathed his gift of a university medal. What hopes did Mary Ann have for her son in a colony where someone like her would never see the inside of a house of learning? Decades later my father went to school barefoot, but at least he went.

Would it be some consolation to both the ghost of my great-great-grandmother and the ghost of Wentworth that they now meet on these pages? Wentworth helped found The University of Sydney 'to enlighten the mind, to refine the understanding, to elevate the souls of our fellow men' (Tink, 2009) and he was also the first Australian-born to publish a book. Perhaps he would be proud that my great-great-grandmother's descendant should have the opportunity to ponder one of his, and my, great passions: the published word.

And what a passion books can be. Book lovers see their relationships with books like a great romance: 'I couldn't put it down', 'it was a good read', 'a real page-turner'. Whether your passion is passion itself—from the fripperies of cheap romance to the lovelorn woes of Emily Brontë—or historical writings told in such a way that you are on the battlefield or in the *palazzo*, the future of books is as assured as history itself. The romance with books will continue even though the look and feel of books will change, and for semi-Luddites like me, it will take a bit of getting used to.

The written word will be relegated to bits and bytes rather than pages. We will lose touch with touch, another sense in our reading journey. We will lose a sense of place (I can't see when I'm halfway through a book on an electronic reader) and, like my ancestors' connection with the land, the connection of books to nature will disappear. There was once life in their pages: the pulp from whence books come, the papyrus, the rice paper, the silk, the stone—all gone. The silicon of the chip and the petrochemical casing seem too far removed from the natural world to harbour the same sensuality as a well-published spine.

Perhaps Wentworth would not be so concerned about the physical change to books but moreso with our local version of a 'war' on books. The first Australian to be published might well be incensed at the threat to territorial copyright for our own dear writers. This copyright prevents dumpage of low-royalty book stock in Australia, effectively protecting our writers' income; our writers' rights. It's a different kind of threat to books: the threat of the bland; the threat to our voice; the threat to a literature unique to us which can only be sustained through nurture, not through the banality of business interests. Or, as Richard Flanagan (2009) so aptly puts it, 'what nation can advance with its tongue torn out?' There is still hope, though, that the free market will not prevail in this instance and that temperance will win. That politicians will see the argument for protection of Australian writers' rights as an imperative, rather than the lackadaisical yearnings of the chattering classes.

Would Wentworth be surprised at the changing view of the published word, or might he be pleased at the prospect of digital download to phones, to computers, to e-book readers, to any electronic device with a readable screen? Five centuries after Gutenberg's press there is gutenberg.org, created to distribute free e-books to all. Centuries before Christ there were plant, animal and mineral inks, and now we have e-ink, a computerised version made to replicate the reading experience on book readers like Kindle. E-ink—composed of millions of microcapsules and no thicker than the human hair—attempts to replicate real ink, and the devices on which it works have no backlighting. This means they may be read in the sun or even childlike at night, cocooned under the bedcovers with a torch. Manufacturers have gone to lengths far to imitate the paper-reading experience, maybe to give us comfort in our transition. If it's speed you're after, however, the standard PC screen hooked up to the internet is enough. Long gone is the encyclopaedia salesman with his heavyweight tomes and gold-embossed pages of wisdom. Britannica no longer rules; it's now Wikipedia, vast databases, e-journals, scanned pages and PDFs.

What of equity, though, in this new world of online reading and research? For those who have access to technology there is no question that access to e-books is more equitable: easy and cheap and readily available in the home or the public library. To the underprivileged, though, this technology-based learning is inaccessible. As inaccessible as was the Republic of Letters in the Age of Enlightenment, when the book trade was often 'dominated by exclusive guilds, and the books themselves … could not appear legally without a royal privilege and a censor's approbation' (Darnton, 2009). And we cannot deny that, for much of the world, illiteracy is still a plague. The changing form of books is unlikely to remove this scourge and may indeed make it worse. To our shame, remote Indigenous communities in Australia are the worst off in our community with only twenty per cent of students achieving a Year Three literacy benchmark (Storry, 2006). It is unlikely that the changing world of books will be positive for their literacy development, and given the nature of technology in the bush—often unavailable, often unreliable—literacy rates could deteriorate from their meagre starting point.

Is there perhaps an existential angst in my imaginings of books' future? Do the words really exist if they're not on paper? Are the bits and bytes, the ons and offs, the zeros and ones the same as words in ink? Is there such a thing as ephemeral and more ephemeral? I originally wrote this in the low-tech tradition: pen and paper, scribe and scribbler. I am a touch-typist, speedy and accurate, and quite a speedy reader, too; racing to the end but never wanting to cross the finish line of a good book. Though I am generally speedy in most things, it seems appropriate to contemplate the future of books slowly; purposefully. For me, conversing on the future of books is a bit like thinking about death. I didn't exist in the past and it will not be too bothersome if I don't exist in the future. It is only hubris, dumb ego, which gets in the way of such frank thinking. And it is my dumb ego which gets in the way of my thinking about books in any other way except what I have known—paper and ink, bound and shelved. And yet I know, already, that just as death stalks us all, the future stalks books: the nature of books will change, and the death knell rings for traditional publishing. Gutenberg was revolutionary and so is the gadgetry for dissemination of knowledge in a technical world. E-books, electronic readers, mixed media delivery: they are with us now, growing in popularity and signalling the demise of the paperback and the hardback.

My bookshelves will soon look rather quaint. I scan the spines of the countless texts, ungainly stacked in the bedroom bookshelves. I like to have my books close, where I can see them, smell them, touch my history. They make me feel real. I hoard bad books with good, trash with treasure, the rich with the bland, science fiction with science fact, self-help with self-delusion. They are the friends who saw me through illness, break-ups, procrastinations, travels, sleepless nights and dream-inducing slumber. This makes me wonder more about my forebears, bookless since time began.

I do not doubt, dear great-great-grandmother, that your imaginary world was as rich as mine. I know about songlines and the Dreamtime, as ancient as the world itself. I stand in the middle of history: the mid-line between my ancestors and my descendants. Did you, Mary Ann, a woman of the land, imagine your descendant, me, as literate, studious, soft handed (or simply soft)? Did you ever turn the pages of a book and wonder how to access its secrets? Did you imagine me, like I now imagine the future? My granddaughter will not live in a bedroom full of books. Will not use books as I do—as a security blanket to prove knowledge, prove a history, prove a life—unless she has a passion and the pocket for the antique, for the bespoke, or indeed for a few grubby copies of her grandmother's books left over from time past. Perhaps she will keep my signed copy of *People of the Book* or would its bookly worship, that people would risk their lives for a book, seem absurd in a digitised age? Should even this essay survive my mortality and make it into her hands, an essay spanning generations, what would she think of my obsession? Laugh at my predictions and my predilections, or acknowledge herself in me; a lover of the written word, no matter what the format, no matter the way. The privilege of knowledge knows no bounds, just like my maternal love which forms the imaginary granddaughter; a love that will follow her through generations of book-lovers to come. I don't know. I am, perhaps, no great soothsayer. The future, like the past, is slippery and uncertain.

What I can foresee, though, is that the world of books is changing; has already changed, and will change yet further. No traditional library can compete with the digitised version of knowledge. Perhaps it is appropriate that all books be unbound from their earthly status and flung into the ether;

the ethernet, the web (and oh, what a tangled web we weave). 'Googleising' books is underway and all human knowledge will soon be out there, available as long as we can access technology. The romance of the Long Hall in Trinity will be superseded by an invisible repository—books made ethereal, words made ghostlike, the ghost in the machine; *deus ex machina.*

    I can already foresee myself switching off the added extras on my digital book reader. Extras like video, audio, narrated text, witty comments from the author or even author interviews. Random House, for example, will have 2500 titles available online by the end of the year, 'many with "rich" content, these steroidal "super-books" are making a serious play for literary attention and our cash' (Jones, 2009). I, for one, do not want another's imaginings invading my headspace. The thing about a paper book is that it 'looks' different to each person who beholds it. Our mind's eyes are different and all the better for it. I want my own Heathcliff, not someone else's. I still remember the frisson of excitement when my English mistress, Mrs Walsh, allowed me to borrow *Wuthering Heights* at a time when (due to its somewhat salacious nature) it was only available from the seniors' library, and I was but thirteen. She did some fast talking with the librarians and my first literary love affair began. I'm glad that was not an enhanced digital reader, giving me images not my own, for what spawns creativity is imagination and surely our imaginations will be diminished if we are thrown words, image and sound in a media-rich 'book'.

    Given the vagaries of technology, the unreliability of the internet, and the censor's easy access to its pages, the danger lies in its design. Genetic engineering of plants has given rise to seed banks, protecting the purity of stock. Will there be something similar to a preservation bank for books? Prescience would say yes. All knowledge kept safe in its purest form—words on paper; a 'just in case' protection for human knowledge. Imagine if, with the flick of a switch, all books, all knowledge, could be wiped out; gone forever. At least low-tech is stable, reproducible and can be housed in many places at once. The end of books could be the beginning of a new Dark Age, or more horribly a brave new world à la Aldous Huxley, where pleasure lies in a pill and consumer satisfaction. Then again, are we so far from that now?

I think of my ancestors once more: those with an oral history and a rich one, not needing writing for their cultural proliferation. They protected their culture and their knowledge through the song of the spoken word; through art and dance; through long-held ritual; from father to son, mother to daughter—but no written word. Need I worry? Well, there were those who worried before me. While the barbarians sacked Europe, destroying everything—even the written word—in their paths, the Irish monks were transcribing through sweat, blood and tears all available literature (Cahill, 1995). If it weren't for the monks' work, would Western civilisation exist as we know it?

We are social beings, from the cradle to the grave, and books are another way we connect to humanity. Whether it is through the compressed wood we call 'paper' or a marvellous (to some) LCD tablet akin to the stones of old, we shall never be without our connection through words. I watch my young daughter, tummy down, propped by elbows, book in hands, lying in the window seat with a good light and a light breeze fluttering on her softly freckled face. I call her name once, twice, three times. There is no answer. My response is not one of anger at being ignored, but of delight. She is lost, lost like I can be, in the world of a good book. E-ink or ink on paper; it does not matter from whence the words come, for the future of books is in the hands of my child and yours. For where there are readers willing to be lost in a reverie of words, and where there are writers willing to take them there, there will be books.

> 'The love of learning, the sequestered nooks,
> And all the sweet serenity of books.'
> — Henry Wadsworth Longfellow

References
Cahill, T. (1995). *How the Irish Saved Civilization: The Untold Story of Ireland's Heroic Role From the Fall of Rome to the Rise of Medieval Europe*, New York, Doubleday.
Darnton, R. (2009). 'Google and the Future of Books', in *The New York Review of Books,* 12 February.
Flanagan, R. (2009). 'Closing Address', The Sydney Writers' Festival, 24 May.
Jones, C. (2009). 'The Future of Books and Electronic Reading', in *The Sunday Times*, 24 May.
Storry, K. (2006). 'Tackling Literacy in Remote Aboriginal Communities', Issue Analysis, The Centre for Independent Studies [online]. Available: www.cis.org.au/
Tink, A. (2009). *William Charles Wentworth: Australia's Greatest Native Son*, Crow's Nest, NSW, Allen & Unwin.

Acknowledgements

Thank you to the contributors for putting pen to paper, capturing nature through a lens and providing this book with such creative and inspiring pieces. Your talent will continue to grow and we wish you success in the Australian cultural scene.

The Team thanks the Department of Media and Communications and the School of Letters, Art and Media at the University of Sydney for their support with the publication of this anthology. We would also like to acknowledge the invaluable guidance received from Mark Rossiter and Dr Fiona Giles.

We are also grateful to Christian Cuello, Skye Starkey and Nick Wright for their artistic contributions and to James White, Jarod Crowe and Bailey Trinh for their work on the anthology website.

Finally, the Team would like to acknowledge the enthusiasm and kind assistance of the Sydney Uni Co-Op Bookshop.

The Team

Selection
Katherine Fitzpatrick
Stephanie Hawkins
Martina Marsic
Elaine Tse
Vanessa Williams

Editing
Sonia Chan
Brittany Cooper
Rachel Dennis
Georgia Eliades
Carolina Pomilio
Elizabeth Riley
Nicola Santilli

Design
Romina Cavagnola
Elaine Tse
Dale Weber
Vanessa Williams

Proofreading
Brittany Cooper
Tiffanny Junee
Carolina Pomilio
Nicola Santilli

Marketing
Brittany Cooper
Tiffanny Junee
Martina Marsic